Malcolm Lowry

A Preface
to His Fiction

**Richard
K.
Cross**

The
University of Chicago Press
Chicago and London

The University of Chicago Press, Chicago 60637
The University of Chicago Press, Ltd., London
© 1980 by The University of Chicago
All rights reserved. Published 1980
Printed in the United States of America
86 85 84 83 82 81 80   5 4 3 2 1

RICHARD K. CROSS is associate professor of English
at UCLA and the author of *Flaubert and Joyce:
The Rite of Fiction.*

LIBRARY OF CONGRESS CATALOGING IN PUBLICATION DATA
Cross, Richard K 1940-
    Malcolm Lowry: a preface to his fiction.
    Includes index.
    1. Lowry, Malcolm, 1909-1957—Criticism and
interpretation.
PR6023.096Z595   813'.5'4   79-16091
ISBN 0-226-12125-9

*For my mother and father,
and for Christa*

Contents

Preface

More than a decade has passed since I first encountered *Under the Volcano* and found myself drawn into a Sierra Madre of the mind, punctuated by cliffs of fall. Lowry's novel struck me then (and the impression has been confirmed by each subsequent reading) as a work in the tradition of those early twentieth-century masters—Conrad and Joyce, Kafka, Mann, and Proust—whose commitment to a complex symbolic mode did not exclude, but rather deepened, a capacity for the realistic rendering of both psyche and circumstance. A narrower sort of avant-garde writing, the antimimetic, game-playing manner of men like Nabokov, Borges, and Pynchon, has dominated serious fiction in recent years, but this later movement can hardly be said to have taken the place of high modernism. Novels like *Nostromo, Ulysses,* and *Doktor Faustus* clarify the terms of our existence in ways that the newer mode—with its comparative neglect of the relations between the self and the larger world, our common life—has abdicated. The high modernist fusion of symbolism and mimesis has not altogether vanished (Günter Grass seems to me its foremost contemporary practitioner), but *Under the Volcano* is among the few distinguished examples of it to appear since the 1930s. To rank the *Volcano* with the classics of modernism is to imply that Malcolm Lowry is a very important writer indeed. The disparity between his major novel and the rest of his writings qualifies but does not fundamentally alter that judgment.

Most readers will in all likelihood come to this study looking primarily for an elucidation of Lowry's magnum opus, and that is in fact where the stress falls. The interpretation of *Under the*

Volcano in chapter 2, the core of my inquiry, attends both to the mimetic base of the novel and to its symbolic superstructure. My root assumption is that traditional exegesis can, by attending closely to what Stendhal called the *petits faits vrais,* lead us to a clearer perception of those elements, most notably character and plot, that remain at the heart of effective narrative than can more recent structuralist and poststructuralist approaches. These remarks will not, I hope, be construed as a plea for myopic formalism. In dealing with *Under the Volcano,* one must take into account the circumstances of its composition, its relation to the novelist's total *oeuvre,* and its affinities with other works in the modern tradition. The question is one of emphasis. I simply want to underscore what, given the intricacy of the novel's symbolism, is too easily forgotten: many of its depths lie on the representational surface.

Chapters 1 and 3 attempt, on the one hand, to place the *Volcano* within the matrix of Lowry's overall artistic development and, on the other, to assess his stories and lesser novels both in their own right and in relation to the entire corpus of his fiction. In general, my analyses of these works, especially the longer ones, follow the contours of the action, just as my reading of the *Volcano* does, although I have at times diverged from this tack when it interfered with the discussion of paradigmatic features: recurrent themes, constellations of symbols, generic models, elements of the author's private mythology, and the like. This strategy would appear to be obvious enough, but most Lowry criticism has in fact proceeded otherwise, concentrating on the symbolism of his works and tending to neglect their narrative structures. Tangents that seemed worth pursuing, at least a short way, and matters likely to be of interest chiefly to specialists have been relegated to the notes.

The first chapter examines the fiction Lowry wrote in the early and middle 1930s, the period in which he was learning his craft and acquiring the experience that prepared him to compose his major work. The unfinished novella *Lunar Caustic* receives particular attention, since it prefigures so clearly aspects of Lowry's mature style. His efforts during the last ten years of his life to transcend the tragic vision of the *Volcano* and to establish a new domain for his art constitute the matter of chapter 3. The novelist regarded virtually everything he wrote as part of a sequence entitled *The Voyage that Never Ends,* whose scope came almost to resemble that of *A la recherche du temps perdu.* Lowry's aspirations for the *Voyage* are among the marks of his seriousness as a writer, and his failure to attain more than a small portion of them represents a loss beyond reckoning. One of the principal grounds for that failure was the artist's deepening isolation—"self exiled in upon his ego," as Joyce has it in the *Wake*—which led to his becoming less and less capable of rendering the kind of tension between self and world that gives the *Volcano* much of its force. From the standpoint of fiction, then, his predicament may be viewed as a severe attenuation of the mimetic mode that sustains his best work. Even in decline, however, Lowry remains an intriguing figure. Novels like *Dark as the Grave Wherein My Friend Is Laid* or *October Ferry to Gabriola,* deeply flawed in design and far from complete, deserve scrutiny in spite of their shortcomings, for they offer us portals we would not otherwise have into the author's extraordinary labyrinthine consciousness. Several of the stories in *Hear Us O Lord from Heaven Thy Dwelling Place,* which contains Lowry's most fully realized fiction apart from the *Volcano,* center specifically on the quandary indicated above. Perhaps the most memorable of these is "Strange Comfort Afforded by the Profession," in which the difficulties are not merely registered but brought under reasonably firm artistic control. The final piece in the collection, "The Forest Path to the Spring," represents a psychological and formal breakthrough for Lowry. Had he been able to bring the spiritual strength evident in the novella to bear elsewhere in his writing, the 1950s might have become as fruitful a time for him as the early 1940s had been. In any case, the minor fiction, together with the *Volcano,* allows us to infer the approximate shape he intended the *Voyage* to assume. The only works that have been excluded from consideration altogether are the poems. Lowry was by no means without lyric gifts; his talents, however, were those of a poet in prose, and his attempts at verse add very little to either his achievement or our grasp of it.

Anyone treating a writer like Lowry, whose most compelling subject was himself, will find it difficult to avoid investigating links between the novelist's life and his art. Exploration of this nexus has proved most essential in dealing with works like *Dark as the Grave*, which still adhere to the author's psyche, and least so with the *Volcano*, where the navel cord has been severed. The psychological analyses focus, for the most part, on Lowry's characters rather than on his person, although the author's close identification with his protagonists makes strict observance of this distinction impossible. I have not attempted to generate new biographical data but rather to bring the available evidence to bear in ways that illumine the works, which are themselves the most revealing spiritual documents we have. The theme that figures more prominently than any other in the following pages is the drama of self-probing that Lowry enacts in the fiction, his efforts to diagnose and, at least at points, to heal lesions within the self as well as in its relations with others and with the ground of its being.

Lowry scholarship has flourished in recent years (see the appendix for a survey of the principal secondary works). My own lines of interpretation were firmly drawn and a draft of much of this study written before any critical books, except Perle Epstein's *The Private Labyrinth of Malcolm Lowry* (1969), appeared. I have sought to offer interpretations of the fiction, based partly on fresh insights and partly on a more precise formulation of some already current, that either do justice to the narratives in their integrity or explore their failure to attain wholeness; to bring into sharper focus the relations between *Under the Volcano* and the rest of the novelist's *oeuvre;* and to rectify the excessive accent on symbolist readings that has prevailed in Lowry studies. Lowry criticism seems to me at a stage now comparable to that reached by Joyce scholarship twenty years ago, before men like Robert Martin Adams, Richard Ellmann, S. L. Goldberg, and A. Walton Litz succeeded in striking a proper balance between the representational and symbolic elements in the Irish master's work. If the present study contributes to a similar reassessment of Lowry, it will, I feel, have justified itself. While I have much to say to other Lowry scholars, I hope that I have managed to treat matters that will be of concern to a larger audience as well. If I am correct in believing that major novels are not written by minor authors and that *Under the Volcano* is indeed a masterpiece, then students of modern literature must take Lowry into account. It is to them, rather than to a narrow band of specialists alone, that this book is directed.

I should like to thank the many people who have been of assistance. Professors Gerald Jay Goldberg, Albert J. Guerard, Robert S. Kinsman, Richard D. Lehan, A. Walton Litz, Frank D. McConnell, Philip C. McGuire, James E. Miller, Thomas C. Moser, David Thorburn, John Unterecker, and Susan B. Weston read versions either of individual chapters or of the entire study and offered much valuable advice and encouragement. Mrs. Malcolm Lowry has very kindly answered my questions about her husband and permitted me to quote from his unpublished manuscripts and letters. Mrs. Anne Yandle, head of the Special Collections Division, University of British Columbia Library, and the members of her staff were most helpful to me during my visits to Vancouver in 1970 and 1974. I am grateful also to the American Council of Learned Societies, the University of California Regents, and the Committee on Research of the UCLA Academic Senate for grants-in-aid and to the editors and publishers of *Contemporary Literature, Modern Fiction Studies,* and *Modern Philology* for permission to reprint portions of the following study that appeared, in considerably different form, in their pages. My greatest debt is to my wife, Christa Wolf Cross, who on many occasions took time from her own work to help with mine.

1
Voyages of Self-Discovery

The Apprentice Fiction

It is too often forgotten that man is impossible without imagination, without the capacity to invent for himself a conception of life, to "ideate" the character he is going to be. Whether he be original or a plagiarist, man is the novelist of himself.
                              —José Ortega y Gasset, "History as a System"

[L'artiste] doit, non pas raconter sa vie telle qu'il l'a vécue, mais la vivre telle qu'il la racontera.
                              —André Gide, *Journal*

Malcolm Lowry spoke of his work, a friend recounts, "as though it were a part of his body,"[1] and in a sense it was, for he lived to write and what he wrote was his life. We have to go back to Joyce, who also "wrote over every square inch of...his own body,"[2] to find a novelist in whom experience and art are so intimately joined or, for that matter, one with a comparable belief in his vocation. Conrad Aiken recalls having met no writer more "visibly or happily alight with genius...the more moving, and convincing, and alive, for its very *un*controlledness, its spontaneity and gay recklessness, not to mention its infectiously gleeful delight in itself."[3] Apart from Aiken, few people sensed Lowry's promise prior to the appearance of *Under the Volcano* in 1947, when the author was already thirty-seven years old.

If one judges from the reviews, most early readers of the *Volcano* assumed that Lowry was making his debut as a novelist. Indeed the artist himself seems to have wished that were the case.

In 1933 he had published a novel of the sea, *Ultramarine,* but he came to regard that book, "which set out to be good, [as] an inexcusable mess"[4] and seldom spoke of it without remarking a desire to rewrite it. Except for two short stories, "Hotel Room in Chartres" and "In Le Havre," both of which appeared in 1934, there had been nothing to remind the world of letters that Malcolm Lowry existed.

The long silence did not stem from inactivity. Besides *Under the Volcano,* on which he worked for the better part of nine years, Lowry wrote several versions of the novella *Lunar Caustic* and a thousand-page draft of a novel called *In Ballast to the White Sea.* The artist conceived of these works as a trilogy modeled on Dante's *Commèdia,* in which the *Volcano* was to have been the *Inferno,* a much amplified *Lunar Caustic* the *Purgatorio,* and *In Ballast* the *Paradiso.* This design had to be abandoned when the manuscript and most of the notes for *In Ballast* were lost in a fire that consumed the Lowrys' home in June 1944. Later he came to regard the *Volcano* and *Lunar Caustic,* together with an extensively revised *Ultramarine,* and three or four other novels planned or in progress as parts of a sequence that bore the same title as the earlier trilogy: *The Voyage that Never Ends.*

Of these projects Lowry completed only the *Volcano,* although a reissue of *Ultramarine,* with minor alterations, and a composite version of *Lunar Caustic* did appear after the author's death, the latter edited by his widow, Margerie Bonner Lowry, and the Canadian poet Earle Birney. One must bear in mind, reading Lowry's posthumous books, that they are only approximations of the novels he meant to write.[5] In *Ultramarine* and *Lunar Caustic* as they stand the genius of which Aiken speaks throws off occasional sparks, but there is little doubt that these works repay one's attention chiefly for the light they cast on the artist's imaginative and moral growth. In them and, to a lesser extent, the two short stories and the surviving notes for *In Ballast to the White Sea* one can trace the discovery of theme and technique as well as the increase in self-knowledge that enabled him to begin work on his chef d'oeuvre.

Ultramarine grew out of the novelist's experience as a deck-hand aboard a freighter bound for China. There was never a question of his pursuing a career in the merchant marine; he meant from the outset to use what he learned at sea as grist for his writing. The voyage was inspired by his reading of O'Neill's early plays, and indeed one can hear echoes of *The Hairy Ape* in Lowry's rendering of seamen's dialogue. He acknowledged his kinship with O'Neill and with the author of *Two Years before the Mast* by naming his protagonist Eugene Dana Hilliot. Dana's last name, which the Cockney sailors aboard his ship pronounce 'Illiot, is perhaps an oblique tribute to T. S. Eliot, whose star was rising over Cambridge while Lowry was a student there. "I wish. I were—what?" Prufrock-Dana asks. "A pair of ragged clauses scuttling between two dark parentheses?"[6] No wonder he feels himself to be living inside "inverted commas." The artist's more profound debts, to Conrad Aiken and Nordahl Grieg in particular, are less clearly indicated.

Both the journey to the Orient and the novel based upon it were, on one level, Lowry's means of asserting his independence from the Cheshire family into which he had been born but in which he never felt at home. His father, a prosperous cotton-broker, expected his sons to enter the family firm and sought to educate them accordingly. That Malcolm, at eighteen, preferred the sea to Cambridge left Arthur Lowry at a loss. Still less was he prepared to sympathize with his son's decision to become a writer.[7] The exigencies of the young man's temperament and talent were strong enough to sustain him in his calling, but they could not prevent him from experiencing a sharp sense of guilt at having turned away from his burgher heritage. He spoke, while he was composing *Ultramarine,* of wanting alternately "to kill Liverpool and [him]self."[8]

Given the impasse in Lowry's relations with his family, it was natural for him to seek out surrogate fathers who could accept him as he was and, at the same time, serve as models for the fuller selfhood to which he aspired. In Conrad Aiken he found the first of these mentors. Aiken's *Blue Voyage* appeared in 1927, the year of Lowry's journey to the Orient. The latter discovered the novel upon his return and saw in its form the perfect crystallization of his experience at sea. More than twenty years later he recalled: "I was practically of the opinion that the book was not only dedicated to me, but that I'd written it myself."[9] His admiration for *Blue Voyage* led to an exchange of letters with its author that resulted in Aiken's agreeing to act as guardian and tutor to the younger writer, an arrangement that the latter's bewildered parents accepted with relief. Lowry arrived at the poet's home in Massachusetts with a mass of notes for his first novel, which the two of them worked on together during the summer of 1929. Aiken's influence is evident in the motifs, diction, prose rhythms, wit and, above all, the narrative method of *Ultramarine*. Even the title seems an echo of *Blue Voyage*.[10] The relationship of the two—in Aiken's phrase—"symbiotic sailmakers" grew more involved over the ensuing decade, until finally Lowry's insistence that the "son" was destined to absorb his "father," that it was the older man's fate "simply to become a better 'you' in me,"[11] produced such acute tension that they were compelled to draw back from one another.

Lowry's ties with Nordahl Grieg were only slightly less complicated and nearly as decisive. His identification with Benjamin Hall, the protagonist of *The Ship Sails On,* led him into severe trouble, for his own work in progress came more and more to resemble Grieg's novel. "Much of *Ultramarine,*" he told the Norwegian writer, "is paraphrase, plagiarism, and pastiche from you."[12] Lowry's concern about his supposed lack of honesty was essentially groundless. The two novelists' rendering of life at sea is informed by a common lyric passion, and aspects of the plot and characterization of *Ultramarine* do in fact appear to derive from *The Ship Sails On.* But these features of Lowry's book, however much they may owe to Grieg, are sufficiently colored by the author's style and insights that they become his own. One can hardly describe *Ultramarine* as markedly original, but then few novels by writers in their early twenties are. In Lowry's mind, though, the influence of Grieg posed a serious threat to his integrity. Consequently, in the summer of 1930 he signed on a freighter bound for Norway, hoping that a face-to-face encounter with the older novelist would help him to resolve the problem. As it happened, Grieg was also going through a period of self-questioning, and the meeting with his young admirer had the effect of shoring up the faith of both artists in their powers. The journey to Norway not only gave Lowry courage to continue with *Ultramarine* but also furnished him with the major theme for *In Ballast to the White Sea.*

Midway in *Ultramarine* the hero explains why it would be pointless for him to record his experiences: "What I could achieve would be that usual self-conscious first novel, . . . of which the principal character would be no more and no less, whether in liquor or in love, than the abominable author himself" (U96). In fact, the distance between the writer and his persona, never very great in Lowry's books, is in this one almost nil. That does not mean the result is mere "diarrhoea scribendi," as Dana Hilliot fears, but rather that the key to the novel's significance lies in the search for identity. "Could you still believe in . . . the notion that my voyage is something Columbian and magnificent?" asks Dana. "Very well, then, prepare to be disillusioned, for, like Melville, I shall strip my motive like an onion down to the innermost bulb of degradation" (U99). Clearly he is never more the voyager than when he seeks thus to confront his essential being. In his later work Lowry speaks of a Columbian Adam whose aim is to make his way through the accumulated layers of self-estrangement to the *terra perdita* of paradise.

Since Dana is temperamentally ill-suited to the bourgeois world in which he has been reared, it is natural that he should begin the quest for his proper self with a change of milieu. The discovery that shipboard life is every bit as stratified and nearly as repressive as the public school he has left comes as a bitter disappointment. His efforts to gain acceptance by the crew meet with repeated rebuffs, for the latter are only too aware of the differences in class and education that separate a "toff" who has come to sea to widen his experience from those who follow it out of harsh necessity. Furthermore, custom demands that a boy on his initial passage be subject to strenuous trials until he prove himself a trustworthy shipmate, and these Dana finds it hard to endure. Awkward, baffled by machinery, good for little besides chipping paint, he is simply not a very able mariner. Most painful of all is his rejection by the tattooed cook Andy, whom he regards as "the sort of man to be" (U15), a potential Queequeg to his Ishmael. In these circumstances, Dana becomes more conscious than ever that he lacks a secure mooring.

Winning his comrades' esteem will, he believes, justify him to his girl Janet, "star to the wandering ship" (U27) and coy mistress in this quest romance. That supposition involves him in a dilemma, for she represents precisely those social distinctions he has sought to leave behind in England but which continue to block his entrance into the fraternity of the sea. The question of fidelity to her inevitably entails another of loyalty to his parents and their values. That he still longs for their approval becomes obvious when letters arrive from his mother and Janet. His mother's curt note expresses the hope that Dana is "comfortable and keeping *clean,* because I don't want my son coarsened by a lot of hooligans." Very much the chastened child, he reflects: "She doesn't love me.... What's the use of anything?" (U97). The unconscious link between Janet and his mother reveals itself when he subsequently refuses to read his girl's missive and indeed loses it for a time, much as Geoffrey Firmin misplaces Yvonne's letters in *Under the Volcano.*

Dana anticipates the Consul's disposition alternately to idealize and to degrade women. The former's vision of Janet approaches mariolatry. Once, after a humiliating experience, he fears that he has become unworthy of her. "Yet if he could only see her at this moment," he thinks, "she would give him another chance, she would be so gentle and companionable and tender. Her hands would be like sun gently brushing away the pain" (U26). Janet seems more nearly a sister than a lover, and one is not surprised to learn that there has been no physical consummation. Dana attempts to place the responsibility for this fact on her wish to remain pure, but in his heart he knows that it is attributable equally to his own inhibition. Raised in a family whose watchword was "thou shalt not," he is in consequence "afraid of living, afraid of manhood" (U31).

The young Geoffrey Firmin in the Hell Bunker scene of the *Volcano* is characterized as "a virgin to put it mildly,"[13] an apt description of Dana as well. Both protagonists are syphilophobic, and it is evident that the disease has for them overtones of moral retribution. The fear of infection restrains them from appeasing their physical desires by having sex with prostitutes. When the Consul ultimately yields to the temptation, he does so not because he expects satisfaction but rather to avenge himself on his former wife and to confirm his self-damnation. Dana manages to resist till the end, but a comparable resentment of Janet and the norms for which she stands plays an important part in his fascination with the demimondaines he encounters in Asian ports. His abortive rendezvous with the Russian call girl Olga in Tsjang-Tsjang prefigures Geoffrey's fateful assignation with María at the Farolito. That so many of the details in Lowry's rendering of the erotic theme appear to have been drawn from *The Ship Sails On* probably reflects the author's relative innocence at the time he was composing *Ultramarine*. The characterization of Yvonne in *Under the Volcano*, which rests on the experience of two marriages, is substantially more convincing than the portrait of Janet; nonetheless, the madonna/whore polarity and the feelings of anxiety and shame that complicate the novelist's relations with women persist.

Like Grieg's hero, Dana imagines that he can break out of the double bind imposed by his desire to justify himself to his girl on the one hand and to his fellow seamen on the other by performing a heroic deed. His first opportunity, the rescue of a carrier pigeon stranded atop the mainmast, is preempted by the Norwegian galley boy. Later when the bird falls into the harbor, Dana hesitates to dive in after it, although he is an excellent swimmer, because he fears the presence of sharks. To a young man whose sense of honor recalls that of Conrad's Jim these incidents assume the character of grave defeats, however bathetic they may seem to the reader. This particular motif looks forward to Hugh Firmin's recovery of a seagull in the *Volcano*. Dana, who shares Hugh's weakness for self-dramatization, discovers that his heroic aspirations only tighten the bind he is in and ends by rejecting the impulse to bravado. "I shall never go down with a ship, unless necessary" (U186), he declares in the last chapter.

One means of release Dana does allow himself is alcohol. If it is impossible for him to find solace in brothels, like Andy and many of his other shipmates, he can at least take refuge in bars. The protagonist of *Ultramarine* is, as he has foreseen, a mirror image of his creator in liquor as in love. Among the notes for *In Ballast to the White Sea* is one remarking on the "mother significance" of drink.[14] The novelist refers, it would seem, not just to the oral gratification the drinker experiences but also to the sense of buoyancy he acquires, as though he were afloat on an amniotic sea in which the conflict between society and instinct dissolves. In Lowry's later works this ecstatic state borders on mystical consciousness, what Freud terms "oceanic feelings." Unfortunately, for Dana Hilliot the respite from social pressure is short-lived. The hope that through drinking he might prove his manliness collapses when members of the crew ridicule his inability to hold his liquor. And whatever satisfaction he gets from defying the precepts of his teetotaling parents dissipates the morning after into a remorseful hangover.

The most effective relief Dana is able to obtain comes in those solitary moments when he feels himself at one with the natural world, particularly when he has a sense of being caught up in the movement of water as he does in the following passage: "The ship rose slowly to the slow blue combers, a ton of spray was flung to leeward, and that other sea, the sky, smiled happily down on her, on seamen and firemen alike, while a small Japanese fishing boat glimmered white against the black coast—oh, in spite of all, it was grand to be alive!" (U23). For some readers these rhapsodic rhythms serve to explain Aiken's wry suggestion that the young writer call his book *Purple Passage,* but for Lowry himself the eroticized perception of the world they embodied was a much needed antidote to repression.

By turning to the sea Dana rediscovers, in Joyce's phrase, the "mighty mother" of us all. She calls him back to an awareness of what lies at the core of his being and reminds him that he has as much right as any other creature to fulfill himself. From this assurance emerges Dana's readiness to challenge his antagonists in the social sphere. Having taken the initial step of leaving his parents' house, he must proceed to the next and transcend surrogates. Rather than permit the expectations of others to determine his identity, he has, in his imagination, to construct a lineage from which the "I" he wishes to become can be born. Out of the range of potential selves implicit in the psyche he alone must make the ultimate choice. Or, as he affirms: "It is I who am the father, or who would be the father, the mother, and who postulate the responsibility for both" (U102). In *Ulysses* Stephen Dedalus makes essentially the same claim for the power of the artist, as "the father of all his race,"[15] to reinvent the terms of his existence.

When Dana finally confronts his chief tormentor, Andy, the latter relents and eventually calls him "son." The protagonist welcomes this paternal overture, but he has already begun to recognize Andy's limitations, specifically his lack of tenderness toward women and his inability to penetrate beyond a very narrow circle of experience. "I *am* Andy," he declares. "But I have outgrown Andy. Mentally, I have surrounded Andy's position, instead of being baffled and hurt by it" (U185). Dana is far from having settled his erotic problems, but at least he understands that they cannot be resolved by emulating the cook's misogynous sensuality.

In the euphoric moments following his discovery that he must father his own identity if it is to be authentic, Lowry's hero underestimates the breach that separates the insight from its realization. Aside from an impulse to serve others, a dream like Hugh Firmin's of "changing the world...through his actions" (V9), Dana has no idea what the basis of this new selfhood will be. But he is surely correct in thinking that the "I" he wishes to become can be attained only by an outward reach of love, by acting in a way that transforms himself and his culture at the same time. It is, of course, an extraordinarily difficult project, and one that has scarcely begun as *Ultramarine* ends. In his first novel Lowry merely broaches the question of identity to which he returns in all his subsequent writings.

Ultramarine anticipates not only several of the major themes and personages of the *Volcano* but also aspects of its narrative strategy. Lowry appropriates from Aiken the counterpointing of syncopated dialogue and interior monologue. The smoking-room episodes in *Blue Voyage,* with their juxtaposed conversations that bear on one another only in tangential fashion, are echoed in the fo'c'sle scenes of Lowry's book. Aiken has a finer ear than his disciple; nevertheless, the latter's dialogue, even when it appears forced and flat, does manage to suggest the isolation from which his characters suffer and the difficulty they have in communicating with one another. The fact that the raciness of the mariners' idiom is more effectively rendered toward the end of *Ultramarine* than it is in the earlier chapters indicates the young author's ability to enter increasingly into a world quite different from the one in which he had been reared. Except for George Orwell, Lowry goes perhaps further than any other writer of his generation, which sent so many poet-martyrs to the Spanish War, to ground his art in an acquaintance with working-class life. In any case, Lowry's experiments with syncopated dialogue in his first novel look forward to his considerably more skillful use of the technique in such crucial scenes of *Under the Volcano* as the one in which Yvonne returns to Geoffrey at the beginning of chapter 2 and the final episode in the Farolito.

The most energized writing in *Ultramarine* may be found in those passages that capture the protagonist's inward life, and indeed throughout the novelist's career his forte remained the depiction of mental processes. Hilliot's meditations concerning Janet, the sea, his boyhood experiences, and the identity he is seeking occur typically as extended parentheses in the fo'c'sle dialogue. Often they are elaborated into imagined scenes more vividly realized than any of those that represent overt action. At the end of chapter 1, for example, Dana, his brain saturated with gin, drifts off to sleep amid a swirl of impressions:

> Then he was walking again with Janet, slowly, through the crowd. Electric lights swam past. Gas jets, crocus colored, steadily flared and whirred. . . . All at once, every lamp in the street exploded, their globes flew out, darted into the sky, and the street became alive with eyes; eyes greatly dilated, dripping dry scurf, or glued with viscid gum: eyes which held eternity in the fixedness of their stare: eyes which wavered, and spread, and, diminishing rapidly, were catapulted east and west; eyes that were the gutted windows of a cathedral, blackened, emptiness of the brain, through which bats and ravens wheeled enormously, leathern foulnesses, heeling over in the dry winds: but one eye plunged up at him from the morass, stared at him unwinkingly. It was the eye of a pigeon, moist and alone, crying. Where would he die? At sea! His body buoyed by slow sustained suspension, pushed at by sea strawberries and sea sponges and fiddler crabs. Coiling and heaving, buzzing and falling. Humus for the sea-polyps, for the ocean-storming behemoth. (U44)

In its interweaving of the motifs of guilt, longing, and fear of death, Dana's revery recalls analogous passages in *A Portrait of the Artist,* especially those that evoke Stephen's nighttown experience and its aftermath.[16] The stylistic richness and psychological depth of the interior monologues, as compared with the seamen's talk or the scenes of action, point to a critical fissure in the author's being. Despite Lowry's recognition that a proper identity could be achieved only through acting in the world, the pain and difficulty entailed in following that path cause him to draw back into narcissistically oriented consciousness. He dramatizes this conflict most effectively in the opposition of Hugh and Geoffrey Firmin in *Under the Volcano.*

Ultramarine allows us to chart the development of a writer whose apprenticeship was coming to a close and who showed considerable promise as a stylist. It is difficult to imagine, though, how Lowry could have recast the book to make it a worthy companion to the *Volcano* in *The Voyage that Never Ends,* as he wished to do. He told his editor, Albert Erskine, that half the lines in the original version should be canceled, contending that *Ultramarine* was "essentially a short novel,"[17] and indeed most of the changes in the posthumous edition involve deletions. But the central flaws of the novel are embedded in its very design and reflect the author's immaturity at the time of its conception. These problems cannot be remedied simply by cutting or by rewriting passages here and there. Probably the most satisfactory disposition of the material in *Ultramarine* was the use to which Lowry put it in the *Volcano,* that is, investing Hugh Firmin with a seafaring past similar to Dana Hilliot's. That the novelist himself saw Dana as a precursor of Hugh is suggested by one of the few substantive alterations in the 1962 edition. In the earlier version Dana's ship is called the *Nawab* and in the later one the *Oedipus Tyrannus,* the name of the freighter that awaits Hugh in Vera Cruz and that is to take him on an arms-running mission to the Spanish Loyalists. The latter name may strike some readers as contrived, but it does at least conform with Dana's will to become his own father.[18]

In the year following the appearance of his first book Lowry wandered from London to Granada to Paris. While he was visiting with Aiken in Spain, the latter introduced him to a young American named Jan Gabrial, hoping she would divert him from the cantina-crawling that had already become a serious threat to his equilibrium. That Aiken's matchmaking was not altogether charitable becomes clear in *Ushant,* where the poet admits that he was himself attracted to Jan and sought, by handing her on to his surrogate son, to indulge in a species of "voyeur's incest." The scheme worked, at least to the extent that the younger man was enchanted by the girl, whose name made the imaginary Janet of *Ultramarine* seem prophetic of a joy he might actually experience. They were married in Paris several months after their initial meeting; however, the happiness they found in the early days of their relationship—the Consul recalls the unalloyed hopes of that time during his last desperate moments—could not endure. Lowry was still too much involved in the emotional conflicts engendered by his family history to form a stable alliance with any woman. The guilt stemming from defiance of his parents' mores made anything more than transient satisfaction impossible at this stage. He remained, as he said to Aiken, "a small boy chased by furies."[19]

Lowry's ambivalence toward his first wife lies at the heart of two short stories from this period, "Hotel Room in Chartres" and "In Le Havre," which prefigure in a number of significant details the theme of marital discord in *Under the Volcano.* In "Hotel Room in Chartres," as in all Lowry's works, "the world is a forest of symbols."[20] Baudelaire's phrase seems especially apposite to a story that opens in Paris on a "spring morning with wavering clouds of rain, like smoke, and . . . everywhere the smoke, smoke from factory chimneys, blown and torn by the wind" (P19). This vision awakens no feeling of renewal in the unnamed protagonist but instead reminds him of a desolate seascape in which the Eiffel Tower assumes the appearance of a lighthouse. The hero, an ex-boatswain, associates the sea with a life of liberated impulse and Paris with the constraints of marriage. In the former he has glimpsed an elusive something that is at once supremely desirable and unattainable: "he had left the sea, no longer able to endure the pain of its reality, as now without the presence of that reality he could no longer endure the pain of its illusion" (P19). At the same time, he wishes to heal the breach that has developed between his wife and himself.

This reconciliation he hopes to achieve by making a pilgrimage to Chartres, where they had become lovers. His plan is frustrated, first by the weather and then by a domestic quarrel, after which he leaves for the cathedral town alone, hoping his wife will decide to join him en route. Yet when she does, he treats her coldly. Cruelty and compassion, aggressiveness and the reparative urge, follow each other in a seemingly endless cycle. One finds the same pattern in Geoffrey Firmin's relations with Yvonne: the tenderness and the remorse engendered by past failures that dominate his feelings toward her when she is absent yield to a desire to wound when she returns to him.

On the train to Chartres the protagonist of "Hotel Room" encounters four French sailors, who come to represent the camaraderie of the sea for which he pines. The mariners are naturally lusty but restrained in the presence of his wife, whether out of a sense of courtesy or of discomfort one cannot tell. As the journey continues, the hero identifies more and more with the seamen and withdraws from his spouse, until by chance he discovers that they are not headed for a ship, as he had thought, but are instead going back to their families, excited by the prospect of being reunited with them. This disclosure effects an almost miraculous reversal in his emotional stance; land and sea, marriage and freedom, are in an instant reconciled. Because he can see that the sailors regard Brest, where their families dwell, as their proper home, it becomes possible for the young husband to view the arrival of himself and his wife in Chartres as a homecoming too.

Leaving the railway coach, "the station seemed to him like a huge ship being dismantled. Coming out they saw the cathedral, its roof the configuration of a green wave, falling along the tall erratic it seems he must be looking for, rather than trying to remember something. Or perhaps, like the poor cat who had lost an eye in a battle, he is just looking for his sight?" (P259). What he seeks, although he cannot know it, is a return to consciousness of the instinctual vitality repressed in childhood. If one compares him to a cat that has lost its eye, its sight—"I" and insight, in the sailor's case—the cat should be named, like Quincey's tom in the *Volcano,* "Oedipuss."

Plantagenet's voluntary entrance into a psychiatric hospital seems an instance of the child's longing to be cared for, an abdication of adult responsibility. But if he desires a love that comforts and protects, Bellevue, whose door shuts behind him "with the dithering crack of a ship going on the rocks" (P261),[33] is an unlikely spot to search for it. The psychiatric ward, with its harsh regime, seems less a place where the deranged may be cured than one where they are punished for the sins of civilization; indeed the hospital is itself a microcosm of the diseased society that surrounds it. Plantagenet feels that he has "voyaged downward to the foul core of his world" (P279), deep into the darkness at the heart of both his own neurosis and the nightmare of culture. He anticipates the Consul's intuition that one can hope to rise from the abyss only after having plumbed its depths.

In the course of his descent Plantagenet learns that Eros has been displaced into things, that the death instinct has turned urban existence into a "mechanic calamity." One evening as he gazes out over the city a seaplane gliding "whitely" past the window of his ward appears to have "the fins and flukes and blunt luminous head of a whale" (P303). When a moment later this "phantom destroyer" seems about to collide with the building, Plantagenet, who at first identifies himself to hospital authorities as the S.S. *Lawhill,*[34] imagines that he is a ship breaking up. Progress has transformed both the man and his onetime blood-and-sperm adversary into machines. Unfortunately Bill's perception that society as a whole shares his malady,

rock of the spire, the blue and white sea of the cool sky rushing behind. . . . The moon drew softly the outgoing tide of the woman towards the calming sea of the man" (P24). Water, rock, spire, and moon are plainly Lawrentian images of sexual union, and indeed the story closes with husband and wife enfolded in each other's arms in the very room on the ruelle de la Demi-Lune where their love had begun. That the hotel should be situated on a *ruelle* suggests a possible origin of the name Laruelle in *Under the Volcano,* although another meaning of *ruelle,* the gap between bed and wall, is perhaps more to the point in Jacques's case. Laruelle too draws a parallel between his passion for a woman and the spell of Chartres, "whose every sidestreet he had come to love. . .where he could gaze at the Cathedral eternally sailing against the clouds" (V12).

The peace that Laruelle has found in his love for Yvonne Firmin proves transient, and the resolution that the two lovers attain in the final lines of "Hotel Room" appears precarious as well. It is unstable because life consists not just of symbols, as the hero supposes, but also of the objects, instincts, and experience that they mediate. In the case of one whose relationship to his world is so tenuous, the result is all too predictable. "Chartres," he thinks, "was his wife, his very blood" (P20). Unfortunately the equation is spurious. Chartres and his wife are only shadows of that Other with which, at the center of his being, he desires reunion. For that reason the protean sea—or, rather, what the sea symbolizes—is bound to resume its call.[21]

"Hotel Room" seems to have been a preliminary sketch for chapter 1 of *In Ballast to the White Sea.* Lowry's surviving notes for the lost novel indicate that the protagonist and his wife were to have consciously regarded Chartres as an escape, a temporary truce in the "revolt against their own sexual happiness." In a long letter describing the plot and theme of *In Ballast,* the author relates that his hero "becomes consumed with an absolute passion—in one sense hereditary—to return to the sea. The sea begins to rise within him, haunts his dreams, and this longing elected for himself. One of the rewards, he hoped, would be a fiction through which the "odd but splendid din"[27] of Bix's horn might sound.

Plantagenet is probably speaking for the author when he speculates that it may have been less his wife than "America [he] was in love with" (P266). Legend has it that when the novelist came to the United States in 1934 the customs inspector in New York discovered that his principal piece of luggage was a copy of *Moby-Dick*. His sense of kinship with Melville depended, Lowry once remarked, on such "romantic" correspondences as their having both sailed before the mast, on his having had a grandfather who went down with the windjammer he captained, and on the American writer's having had a son named Malcolm "who simply disappeared."[28] Lowry was, of course, mistaken about Malcolm Melville's "disappearance"; the young man died by his own hand under mysterious circumstances, as his namesake was to do ninety years later. Given the English novelist's mystical belief in coincidence, this last detail may be less trivial than it seems. One should not, in any case, overlook the identification with Melville's son, since filial ties with older writers played such a vital role in his quest for selfhood.

More important than these affinities, however, was Lowry's conviction that there existed an ominous parallel between Melville's career and his own: "His failure for some reason absolutely fascinated me and . . . from an early age I determined to emulate it, in every way possible."[29] In this conception of the artist as a failure in the world's eyes—and, all too often, in his own as well—lies the real romantic bond between the two men. Both were riven by the demonic urge to liberate their hidden selves and the counterpressure of society and conscience.[30] That they wrote *Moby-Dick* and *Under the Volcano* while they were still in their thirties and never again approached the mark set by their *opera maxima* underscores the toll this split exacted. The last decade of Lowry's life, with its weight of money troubles, illness, and still-

born works, in every way rivals the abyss of Melville's yea custom house.

Lowry's experience of New York crystalized in a wor original title, *The Last Address*, refers to the site, near E where *Moby-Dick* was completed, and the story is in fact a man's hysterical identification with Melville."[31] In 7 *Address*—or *Lunar Caustic*, as the novella came to be cal protagonist walks the city streets as though he were Ahab bling from side to side on the careening bridge, 'feeling encompassed in his stare oceans from which might be that phantom destroyer of himself' " (P260). Lowry sha ville's belief that "some certain significance lurks in all t as well as his radical skepticism about the possibility of precisely what that significance is. The two novelists' with epistemological problems is of course the seal of t dernity. They challenged the opacity of the world with weapon their vocation afforded, the imagination, at t time questioning its efficacy, for they had no assura meaning inhered in the objects they contemplated. "Isola off from any firm sanction, metaphysical or moral, for t both feared that they were falling victim to their own pro Given this set of mind, even the minutiae of daily life appallingly ambiguous.

Neon advertisements and tabloid headlines, emblems ture out of joint, confront Bill Plantagenet in the first inconclusive encounters with his "own white whale," outer and inner forces that menace his sanity. New Y bodies for him, as Mexico does for Geoffrey Firmin, horrors of war" (P289). The opening paragraph comp protagonist emerging from a dockside saloon to a ship port, an apt analogy since he appears very much at drunken sailor's wandering is not so aimless as the rea initially suppose, however, for the narrator subseque scribes it as a "pilgrimage," albeit a strange one: "his co useful though it may be as a diagnostic premise, offers little ground for therapeutic optimism.

Plantagenet responds to the dehumanizing forces by retreating into alcoholic isolation and endeavoring to create a hermetic realm, an "inner Africa," that will provide shelter from the demands of a hostile world. Since his ego has been shaped by the tension between instinct and environment, however, such auto-erotic defenses cannot resolve the predicament in which he finds himself. He can begin to integrate his personality only by acting to change conditions both within and outside himself, as Dana Hilliot has in his groping fashion recognized. All of Plantagenet's attempts to establish ties of affection end in frustration. Both his marriage and the jazz combo of which he was the leader have collapsed. His failure as a pianist he attributes to the fact that his hands will not stretch an octave, but the explanation rings counterfeit. When he tries to establish communion with his fellow inmates by playing a medley of jazz pieces, the blacks among his audience reject the overture, preferring to sing themselves. One of them asks Bill whether he can "truck," that is, back up another man's solo.[35] But supporting roles, those in which he cannot control the action, do not appeal to him. "Perhaps," remarks the psychiatrist, "it was your heart you couldn't make stretch an octave" (P266). Plantagenet reacts against the culture that represses him by seeking to dominate any relationship he enters into and by withdrawing when he cannot do so.[36]

Bill's sympathy with the senile Kalowsky and the young schizophrenic Garry, whom he casts in the roles of his father and son, is a healthy sign, an indication of his renewed willingness to risk involvement with other human beings. Even these bonds reflect his need to occupy a superior position, however, for the old man and the boy interest him in large part because he can play doctor with them. His readiness to plead their cases with the Bellevue authorities is in itself admirable, but it has the unfortunate effect of arousing expectations that cannot be redeemed. Bill does obtain the news that Kalowsky is to be transferred from the observation ward to a sanatorium "as soon as it can be arranged" (P292), which, under the circumstances that prevail in the city hospital, may be a long way off. For Garry he is able to do nothing at all; indeed the supervisor chides him for having encouraged the boy's fantasizing. Plantagenet's intervention does little to alleviate the plight of either friend and leaves him more profoundly demoralized than he was at the outset.

It is in his relationship with the psychiatrist, who represents "his last hope, on his final frontier" (P279), that the protagonist experiences his most acute disappointment. Far from being sinewed with malice like his namesake in *Billy Budd,* Dr. Claggart is well-intentioned, overworked, and essentially defeatist concerning his job. At those moments when he finds it possible to think of himself as a therapist and not merely a caretaker, his approach is invariably adjustive, never existential. And that to which the doctor seeks to accommodate his patients—and himself—is not the outside world but rather the psychiatric ward. Plantagenet's belief that mental disturbance may point toward a reorientation of life along more viable lines, that "many who are supposed to be mad . . . are simply people who perhaps once saw, however confusedly, the necessity for change in themselves, for rebirth" (P290), strikes Claggart as evidence that the young man is resisting cure. Everything Bill says the doctor construes as symptomatic of his "morbid" refusal to honor authority. Repression, if it is to be effective, demands that each man execute upon himself the sentence it pronounces, in the manner of Billy Budd. Naturally this compliance is easier to exact when the victim remains unwitting. Not surprisingly, the psychiatrist seems never to have heard of Melville's handsome sailor. Dr. Claggart's capitulation to the order of things as they are renders him a more pathetic figure than many of his patients.[37]

Upon his release from the hospital, Plantagenet enters a church and has the first of many palliative drinks. One remembers the Consul's claim that he imbibes as though he were "taking an eternal sacrament" (V40). A thwarted religious sensibility characterizes the protagonists of both *Lunar Caustic* and *Under the Volcano;* each yearns for a grace that will deliver him from the hell of self-involvement. Unable to find rest in the bosom of mother church, they fall back on alcohol to console themselves. Juxtaposed with the longing for maternal solace is the hostility of Bill and Geoffrey toward most other female forms. Unlike the *Volcano, Lunar Caustic* offers no insight into the childhood experiences of its hero that might account for this split,[38] apart from such stray clues as the fact that the head nurse in Bill's ward evokes memories of his sadistic nanny.

Whatever the underlying grounds for it, Plantagenet's horror at the defilement of Eros becomes especially vivid in the closing paragraphs of the novella. When he hurls an empty flask at the obscene drawing of a woman, he imagines that the protest is directed against the abuses of society, "against all the indecency, the cruelty, the hideousness, the filth and injustice in the world" (P306). At the same time the act calls to mind the reason for Garry's confinement, the killing of a little girl, and compels Bill to acknowledge that destructiveness is inherent in human nature and not merely imposed by external forces. One finds a parallel in the Consul's final quixotic sally against the Unión Militar chiefs, who symbolize the depravity both of society and of the protagonist himself. In Plantagenet's case the quickened awareness of demonic darkness that follows his flinging the bottle unleashes a surge of remorse. It is as though a "terrible old woman," at once Fate and fury, were pursuing him "at the bottom of some mine" (P306). Freud's observation that cultural progress entails a steady intensification of guilt feelings is pertinent: "If civilization is a necessary course of development from the family to humanity as a whole, then—as a result of the inborn conflict arising from ambivalence, of the eternal struggle between the trends of love and death—there is inextricably bound up with it an increase of the sense of guilt, which will perhaps reach heights that the individual finds hard to tolerate."[39] Bill Plantagenet and the heroes of Lowry's later fiction exemplify the truth of that last clause. In the concluding lines of *Lunar Caustic* the protagonist, overwhelmed by the burden he bears, retires "to the very obscurest corner of the bar, where, curled up like an embryo, he could not be seen at all" (P306).

Lunar Caustic in the form that we have it hardly meshes with the novelist's original scheme for *The Voyage that Never Ends,* where, the reader will recall, it was to constitute the *Purgatorio.* [40] For all the talk of rebirth, the suffering Lowry depicts in the novella remains that of the damned rather than those in the process of being redeemed. Only from the standpoint of the Nirvana principle does Plantagenet's symbolic return to the womb represent a triumph. One almost expects to come across a sign in Lowry's New York that reads *A Parián,* for *Lunar Caustic* clearly points the way to the Mexican Inferno. Nowhere is the affinity between the novella and *Under the Volcano* more marked than in the texture of the protagonists' consciousness. The passage in which Plantagenet's agony is compared to "a great lidless eye," for instance, contains unmistakably the germ of a Consular meditation: "The stars taking their places were wounds opening in his being, multiple duplications of that agony, of that eye. The constellations might have been monstrosities in the delirium of God. Disaster seemed smeared over the whole universe. It was as if he were living in the preexistence of some unimaginable catastrophe, and he steadied himself a moment against the sill, feeling the doomed earth itself stagger in its heaving spastic flight towards the Hercules Butterfly" (P267). One discovers an echo in Geoffrey Firmin's apocalyptic musing that "the earth was a ship, lashed by the Horn's tail, doomed never to make her Valparaiso. Or that it was like a golf ball, launched at Hercules' Butterfly, wildly hooked by a giant out of an asylum window in hell" (V287). The witty unfolding of metaphor in the latter quotation illustrates the gain in stylistic power that helps to distinguish the *Volcano* from the more discursive earlier work.

Pressed to provide a sequel to his chef d'oeuvre, Lowry commended *Lunar Caustic* to his editor as "a masterwork, or a potential one."[41] Few readers are likely to second this judgment. As it stands, the novella suffers from such serious defects as the obscurity of its protagonist's motivation, the flatness of its secondary characters, and the ponderousness of much of its symbolism. Lowry might have corrected at least some of these flaws had he been able to devote the six months of additional work to *Lunar Caustic* that would, he claimed, have sufficed to put it in its proper form. It is difficult to resist the conclusion, though, that the novella was never itself a masterpiece-in-embryo but that, like *Ultramarine,* its importance lies in its having prepared the artist to write *Under the Volcano.*

In the same year that he finished the initial version of *Lunar Caustic,* Lowry left New York for Los Angeles, where he evidently hoped to find work as a screenwriter. His Consul compares the "rending tumult" of these cities to the unbandaging of giants. The novelist and his heroes alike remind one of Baudelaire's "matelot ivrogne, inventeur d'Amériques / Dont l'image rend le gouffre plus amer."[42] Lowry remained in California for only a few months and then, with Jan, took ship for Mexico, sailing into Acapulco harbor on the Day of the Dead 1936.[43] "Like Columbus I have torn through one reality and discovered another," declared the artist the following year. "Alas, my only friend is the Virgin for those who have nobody with, and she is not much help, while I am on this last tooloose-Lowrytrek."[44] It was by no means the last of Lowry's perilous voyages, but it was undoubtedly the most decisive, as crucial for him as the journey up the Congo had been for Conrad.

2
Under the Volcano

A Book
of the Dead

There may be in the cup
A spider steeped and one may drink, depart,
And yet partake no venom, for his knowledge
Is not infected. But if one present
The abhorred ingredient to his eye, make known
How he hath drunk, he cracks his gorge, his sides,
With violent hefts. I have drunk, and seen the spider.

—Shakespeare, *The Winter's Tale*

La violence du venim tord mes membres, me rend
difforme, me terrasse. Je meurs de soif, j'étouffe,
je ne puis crier.... Un homme qui veut se mutiler
est bien damné, n'est-ce pas? Je me crois en enfer,
donc j'y suis.

—Rimbaud, *Une saison en enfer*

Lowry cast much of *Under the Volcano* in an apocalyptic-symbolist mode that springs from a correspondence between the "subnormal world" without and the "abnormally suspicious delirious one within him."[1] In order to grasp the reticulation of signs, portents, and motifs one should, the author insisted, read or, better, reread his book, bearing in mind "the poetical conception of the *whole*."[2] That the reader must bring to any given passage an awareness of the pertinent cross-references—its "spatial" design[3]—does not mean, however, that he should regard the book solely in this fashion. One may indeed apprehend a particular segment of Lowry's multilaminate prose in a single moment, but he should remember that each of these elements attains its full significance only as part of a dramatic development. Accordingly, we shall examine the chapters of Lowry's novel in the sequence he ordained. Any drastic rearrangement of the material would not only compromise its effectiveness, he rightly contended, but would also "buckle the very form of the book,...a wheel with twelve spokes, the motion of which is something like that...of time itself."[4]

A Virgil posing as Baedeker leads us into the Mexican *Inferno*. "Two mountain chains traverse the Republic roughly from north to south" (V3), our guide notes and then goes on to offer a matter-of-fact account of the situation and topography of Quauhnahuac, together with information about roads, hotels, places of worship, and recreational facilities likely to be of interest to the tourist. On a first reading one might find such items as the ratio of cantinas to churches curious: only when he returns to this chapter, which serves as both overture and coda, will these particulars gain their proper resonance. Apart from the title of the book and the fact that two volcanoes are said to dominate the valley, there is nothing to suggest the wealth of symbolic meaning that will attach itself to these peaks. Indeed Popocatepetl and Ixtaccihuatl are not even identified for several pages. Similarly, the observation that Quauhnahuac lies on the same parallel as Juggernaut signifies little until we learn that, like the god from whom the town in India takes its name, the old Aztec city has fed on terrible sacrifices. The traveler enters Quauhnahuac, we are told, via a highway that rapidly dissolves into "tortuous and broken" lanes and ends as a goat track. These details prefigure the labyrinthine story about to unfold, the tragedy or "goat-song" of a cuckold, a *cabrón*.[5]

Lowry attached special importance to his mise en scène: the initial chapter sets "the slow melancholy tragic rhythm of Mexico," he declared, "and above all [it] establishes the *terrain*."[6] Having provided us with a panoramic view of Quauhnahuac and the surrounding countryside in his first two paragraphs, the author is ready in the third to bring his theme into sharper focus. A single task remains for the guide: to direct us to one of the "many splendid hotels" in town. The Hotel Casino de la Selva seems an odd choice, for its jai-alai courts are "grassgrown and deserted," the springboards of its pool "empty and mournful," and the gaming tables no longer in operation: "You may not even dice for drinks at the bar. The ghosts of ruined gamblers haunt it." On the hillside behind the Casino, processions of mourners, "visible only as the melancholy lights of their candles" (V4), descend from the cemeteries. We have been conducted into what is, for all its beauty, a wasteland where the presence of the dead is felt more keenly than that of the living.

The story opens on the Day of the Dead (All Souls' Day, 2 November) 1939, two months after the invasion of Poland, with reflections on an event that has taken place exactly one year earlier, an occurrence that "seemed already to belong in a different age. One would have thought the horrors of the present would have swallowed it up like a drop of water. It was not so. Though tragedy was in the process of becoming unreal and meaningless it seemed one was still permitted to remember the days when an individual life held some value and was not a mere misprint in a communiqué" (V5). The reader does not know yet what has happened, but plainly the novelist is preparing him to respond to the account of it with pity and terror.[7] As the preceding meditation indicates, he was acutely conscious of the problem a writer faces in establishing, rather than merely asserting, the tragic status of an action: "it seemed one was still permitted to remember." Tragedy remains a valid mode only if one admits a great deal of ironic qualification. The power and universality of the novel derive to a considerable extent from implicit parallels between the doom that overtakes the principal characters and the horrors of a world at war. Mexico, "pyre of Bierce and springboard of Hart Crane, the age-old arena of racial and political conflicts,"[8] forms a backdrop in every way appropriate to the recounting of psychic battles.

that storms in him day and night...was one of the best parts of the book." All the key terms in this summary confirm the fundamentally erotic character of the blocked emotions. Lowry goes on to say that the "thalassal" impulse, as Sandor Ferenczi terms it, develops into a particular yearning "for the fire of the stokehold, ...the fire in which he sees himself purged and emerging as a reborn man."[22] A similar mystique of the stokehold manifests itself in *The Ship Sails On*—one should remember that the central action of *In Ballast* is the quest for a rapprochement with the father-figure Grieg—and in *The Hairy Ape,* although O'Neill treats the theme with an irony still foreign to Lowry in the pre-*Volcano* period. Clearly *In Ballast to the White Sea* anticipated the preoccupation with redemptive suffering, the dying away of the old self that must precede rebirth, which pervades the artist's mature fiction.

"In Le Havre," the other story that reflects Lowry's unresolved ambivalence toward his first marriage, is thematically less rich than and technically inferior to "Hotel Room in Chartres." The latter represents a modest advance on the method of *Ultramarine* in that the protagonist's monologues have a more intimate connection psychologically with the passages of dialogue from which they flow and to which they return than do Dana Hilliot's. "In Le Havre," consisting entirely of a conversation between a self-involved young Englishman and a case-hardened American newspaperman, reads like a poor pastiche of "Hills like White Elephants."

The Englishman relates that his American bride of five months, Lee, has just sailed for New York on the *Ile de France* in much the same way, apparently, that Jan Lowry had left the author shortly before the story was written. As the ship was about to cast off and the couple were saying their farewells, the husband recounts, he has perversely told his wife: "I don't love you; I never have loved you; it was just a caprice on my part. I married you to satisfy my vanity, I was just getting one back on the old rock of the spire, the blue and white sea of the cool sky rushing behind. . . . The moon drew softly the outgoing tide of the woman towards the calming sea of the man" (P24). Water, rock, spire, and moon are plainly Lawrentian images of sexual union, and indeed the story closes with husband and wife enfolded in each other's arms in the very room on the ruelle de la Demi-Lune where their love had begun. That the hotel should be situated on a *ruelle* suggests a possible origin of the name Laruelle in *Under the Volcano,* although another meaning of *ruelle,* the gap between bed and wall, is perhaps more to the point in Jacques's case. Laruelle too draws a parallel between his passion for a woman and the spell of Chartres, "whose every sidestreet he had come to love...where he could gaze at the Cathedral eternally sailing against the clouds" (V12).

The peace that Laruelle has found in his love for Yvonne Firmin proves transient, and the resolution that the two lovers attain in the final lines of "Hotel Room" appears precarious as well. It is unstable because life consists not just of symbols, as the hero supposes, but also of the objects, instincts, and experience that they mediate. In the case of one whose relationship to his world is so tenuous, the result is all too predictable. "Chartres," he thinks, "was his wife, his very blood" (P20). Unfortunately the equation is spurious. Chartres and his wife are only shadows of that Other with which, at the center of his being, he desires reunion. For that reason the protean sea—or, rather, what the sea symbolizes—is bound to resume its call.[21]

"Hotel Room" seems to have been a preliminary sketch for chapter 1 of *In Ballast to the White Sea.* Lowry's surviving notes for the lost novel indicate that the protagonist and his wife were to have consciously regarded Chartres as an escape, a temporary truce in the "revolt against their own sexual happiness." In a long letter describing the plot and theme of *In Ballast,* the author relates that his hero "becomes consumed with an absolute passion—in one sense hereditary—to return to the sea. The sea begins to rise within him, haunts his dreams, and this longing man,"[23] His motives for marrying Lee and for harassing her remain far from transparent, although in both instances it is plausible that animosity toward his father does indeed play a part. The story offers no direct amplification of the phrase "getting one back on the old man,"[24] but the reader does learn that the son is beset by feelings of unworthiness that seem to prompt his cruelty to Lee and that may well stem from paternal rejection. "We were too happy, too happy, it couldn't last,"[25] he declares, a line the Consul paraphrases in a key meditation almost at the center of the *Volcano* (V201). Like Geoffrey, the young husband wants and does not want his wife, loves her but loves his own misery more. The protagonist of "In Le Havre" in no way approaches the Consul's stature, yet he represents a realm of pain through which Lowry had to pass en route to portraying the hero of *Under the Volcano*.

It was no accident that the artists with whom Lowry felt the strongest affinities were all foreigners. The shaping of a proper identity meant for him viewing his English past through the eyes of outsiders. American writers and musicians particularly suited his purpose, since in the period before World War II they were still less inclined than their European counterparts to feel burdened by history. Bill Plantagenet, the hero of *Lunar Caustic* and, like his creator, a former jazz man, explains his intoxication with certain aspects of life in the New World as follows: "You [Americans] get sentimental over England from time to time. . . . Well, this was the other way round. Only it was Eddie Lang and Joe Venuti and the death of Bix. . . . And I wanted to see where Melville lived. You'll never know how disappointed I was not to find any whalers in New Bedford."[26] That jazz exercised a powerful hold on Lowry is not surprising; more than any other art form it encouraged the spontaneous overflow of Eros, the integral rhythm of body and "soul," for which he yearned. Beiderbecke, who turned from middle-class origins to a career of Dionysian risk taking, seemed a paradigm of the dangerous life he had elected for himself. One of the rewards, he hoped, would be a fiction through which the "odd but splendid din"[27] of Bix's horn might sound.

Plantagenet is probably speaking for the author when he speculates that it may have been less his wife than "America [he] was in love with" (P266). Legend has it that when the novelist came to the United States in 1934 the customs inspector in New York discovered that his principal piece of luggage was a copy of *Moby-Dick*. His sense of kinship with Melville depended, Lowry once remarked, on such "romantic" correspondences as their having both sailed before the mast, on his having had a grandfather who went down with the windjammer he captained, and on the American writer's having had a son named Malcolm "who simply disappeared."[28] Lowry was, of course, mistaken about Malcolm Melville's "disappearance"; the young man died by his own hand under mysterious circumstances, as his namesake was to do ninety years later. Given the English novelist's mystical belief in coincidence, this last detail may be less trivial than it seems. One should not, in any case, overlook the identification with Melville's son, since filial ties with older writers played such a vital role in his quest for selfhood.

More important than these affinities, however, was Lowry's conviction that there existed an ominous parallel between Melville's career and his own: "His failure for some reason absolutely fascinated me and . . . from an early age I determined to emulate it, in every way possible."[29] In this conception of the artist as a failure in the world's eyes—and, all too often, in his own as well—lies the real romantic bond between the two men. Both were riven by the demonic urge to liberate their hidden selves and the counterpressure of society and conscience.[30] That they wrote *Moby-Dick* and *Under the Volcano* while they were still in their thirties and never again approached the mark set by their *opera maxima* underscores the toll this split exacted. The last decade of Lowry's life, with its weight of money troubles, illness, and stillborn works, in every way rivals the abyss of Melville's years in the custom house.

Lowry's experience of New York crystalized in a work whose original title, *The Last Address,* refers to the site, near Bellevue, where *Moby-Dick* was completed, and the story is in fact "about a man's hysterical identification with Melville."[31] In *The Last Address*—or *Lunar Caustic,* as the novella came to be called—the protagonist walks the city streets as though he were Ahab "stumbling from side to side on the careening bridge, 'feeling that he encompassed in his stare oceans from which might be revealed that phantom destroyer of himself'" (P260). Lowry shared Melville's belief that "some certain significance lurks in all things"[32] as well as his radical skepticism about the possibility of defining precisely what that significance is. The two novelists' concern with epistemological problems is of course the seal of their modernity. They challenged the opacity of the world with the only weapon their vocation afforded, the imagination, at the same time questioning its efficacy, for they had no assurance that meaning inhered in the objects they contemplated. "Isolatos" cut off from any firm sanction, metaphysical or moral, for their art, both feared that they were falling victim to their own projections. Given this set of mind, even the minutiae of daily life become appallingly ambiguous.

Neon advertisements and tabloid headlines, emblems of a culture out of joint, confront Bill Plantagenet in the first of many inconclusive encounters with his "own white whale," with the outer and inner forces that menace his sanity. New York embodies for him, as Mexico does for Geoffrey Firmin, all "the horrors of war" (P289). The opening paragraph compares the protagonist emerging from a dockside saloon to a ship leaving port, an apt analogy since he appears very much at sea. The drunken sailor's wandering is not so aimless as the reader may initially suppose, however, for the narrator subsequently describes it as a "pilgrimage," albeit a strange one: "his course is so erratic it seems he must be looking for, rather than trying to remember something. Or perhaps, like the poor cat who had lost an eye in a battle, he is just looking for his sight?" (P259). What he seeks, although he cannot know it, is a return to consciousness of the instinctual vitality repressed in childhood. If one compares him to a cat that has lost its eye, its sight—"I" and insight, in the sailor's case—the cat should be named, like Quincey's tom in the *Volcano,* "Oedipuss."

Plantagenet's voluntary entrance into a psychiatric hospital seems an instance of the child's longing to be cared for, an abdication of adult responsibility. But if he desires a love that comforts and protects, Bellevue, whose door shuts behind him "with the dithering crack of a ship going on the rocks" (P261),[33] is an unlikely spot to search for it. The psychiatric ward, with its harsh regime, seems less a place where the deranged may be cured than one where they are punished for the sins of civilization; indeed the hospital is itself a microcosm of the diseased society that surrounds it. Plantagenet feels that he has "voyaged downward to the foul core of his world" (P279), deep into the darkness at the heart of both his own neurosis and the nightmare of culture. He anticipates the Consul's intuition that one can hope to rise from the abyss only after having plumbed its depths.

In the course of his descent Plantagenet learns that Eros has been displaced into things, that the death instinct has turned urban existence into a "mechanic calamity." One evening as he gazes out over the city a seaplane gliding "whitely" past the window of his ward appears to have "the fins and flukes and blunt luminous head of a whale" (P303). When a moment later this "phantom destroyer" seems about to collide with the building, Plantagenet, who at first identifies himself to hospital authorities as the S.S. *Lawhill,*[34] imagines that he is a ship breaking up. Progress has transformed both the man and his onetime blood-and-sperm adversary into machines. Unfortunately Bill's perception that society as a whole shares his malady, useful though it may be as a diagnostic premise, offers little ground for therapeutic optimism.

Plantagenet responds to the dehumanizing forces by retreating into alcoholic isolation and endeavoring to create a hermetic realm, an "inner Africa," that will provide shelter from the demands of a hostile world. Since his ego has been shaped by the tension between instinct and environment, however, such auto-erotic defenses cannot resolve the predicament in which he finds himself. He can begin to integrate his personality only by acting to change conditions both within and outside himself, as Dana Hilliot has in his groping fashion recognized. All of Plantagenet's attempts to establish ties of affection end in frustration. Both his marriage and the jazz combo of which he was the leader have collapsed. His failure as a pianist he attributes to the fact that his hands will not stretch an octave, but the explanation rings counterfeit. When he tries to establish communion with his fellow inmates by playing a medley of jazz pieces, the blacks among his audience reject the overture, preferring to sing themselves. One of them asks Bill whether he can "truck," that is, back up another man's solo.[35] But supporting roles, those in which he cannot control the action, do not appeal to him. "Perhaps," remarks the psychiatrist, "it was your heart you couldn't make stretch an octave" (P266). Plantagenet reacts against the culture that represses him by seeking to dominate any relationship he enters into and by withdrawing when he cannot do so.[36]

Bill's sympathy with the senile Kalowsky and the young schizophrenic Garry, whom he casts in the roles of his father and son, is a healthy sign, an indication of his renewed willingness to risk involvement with other human beings. Even these bonds reflect his need to occupy a superior position, however, for the old man and the boy interest him in large part because he can play doctor with them. His readiness to plead their cases with the Bellevue authorities is in itself admirable, but it has the unfortunate effect of arousing expectations that cannot be redeemed. Bill does obtain the news that Kalowsky is to be transferred from the observation ward to a sanatorium "as soon as it can be arranged" (P292), which, under the circumstances that prevail in the city hospital, may be a long way off. For Garry he is able to do nothing at all; indeed the supervisor chides him for having encouraged the boy's fantasizing. Plantagenet's intervention does little to alleviate the plight of either friend and leaves him more profoundly demoralized than he was at the outset.

It is in his relationship with the psychiatrist, who represents "his last hope, on his final frontier" (P279), that the protagonist experiences his most acute disappointment. Far from being sinewed with malice like his namesake in *Billy Budd,* Dr. Claggart is well-intentioned, overworked, and essentially defeatist concerning his job. At those moments when he finds it possible to think of himself as a therapist and not merely a caretaker, his approach is invariably adjustive, never existential. And that to which the doctor seeks to accommodate his patients—and himself—is not the outside world but rather the psychiatric ward. Plantagenet's belief that mental disturbance may point toward a reorientation of life along more viable lines, that "many who are supposed to be mad...are simply people who perhaps once saw, however confusedly, the necessity for change in themselves, for rebirth" (P290), strikes Claggart as evidence that the young man is resisting cure. Everything Bill says the doctor construes as symptomatic of his "morbid" refusal to honor authority. Repression, if it is to be effective, demands that each man execute upon himself the sentence it pronounces, in the manner of Billy Budd. Naturally this compliance is easier to exact when the victim remains unwitting. Not surprisingly, the psychiatrist seems never to have heard of Melville's handsome sailor. Dr. Claggart's capitulation to the order of things as they are renders him a more pathetic figure than many of his patients.[37]

Upon his release from the hospital, Plantagenet enters a church and has the first of many palliative drinks. One remembers the Consul's claim that he imbibes as though he were "taking an eternal sacrament" (V40). A thwarted religious sensibility characterizes the protagonists of both *Lunar Caustic* and *Under the Volcano;* each yearns for a grace that will deliver him from the hell of self-involvement. Unable to find rest in the bosom of mother church, they fall back on alcohol to console themselves. Juxtaposed with the longing for maternal solace is the hostility of Bill and Geoffrey toward most other female forms. Unlike the *Volcano, Lunar Caustic* offers no insight into the childhood experiences of its hero that might account for this split,[38] apart from such stray clues as the fact that the head nurse in Bill's ward evokes memories of his sadistic nanny.

Whatever the underlying grounds for it, Plantagenet's horror at the defilement of Eros becomes especially vivid in the closing paragraphs of the novella. When he hurls an empty flask at the obscene drawing of a woman, he imagines that the protest is directed against the abuses of society, "against all the indecency, the cruelty, the hideousness, the filth and injustice in the world" (P306). At the same time the act calls to mind the reason for Garry's confinement, the killing of a little girl, and compels Bill to acknowledge that destructiveness is inherent in human nature and not merely imposed by external forces. One finds a parallel in the Consul's final quixotic sally against the Unión Militar chiefs, who symbolize the depravity both of society and of the protagonist himself. In Plantagenet's case the quickened awareness of demonic darkness that follows his flinging the bottle unleashes a surge of remorse. It is as though a "terrible old woman," at once Fate and fury, were pursuing him "at the bottom of some mine" (P306). Freud's observation that cultural progress entails a steady intensification of guilt feelings is pertinent: "If civilization is a necessary course of development from the family to humanity as a whole, then—as a result of the inborn conflict arising from ambivalence, of the eternal struggle between the trends of love and death—there is inextricably bound up with it an increase of the sense of guilt, which will perhaps reach heights that the individual finds hard to tolerate."[39] Bill Plantagenet and the heroes of Lowry's later fiction exemplify the truth of that last clause. In the concluding lines of *Lunar Caustic* the protagonist, overwhelmed by the burden he bears, retires "to the very obscurest corner of the bar, where, curled up like an embryo, he could not be seen at all" (P306).

Lunar Caustic in the form that we have it hardly meshes with the novelist's original scheme for *The Voyage that Never Ends,* where, the reader will recall, it was to constitute the *Purgatorio.* [40] For all the talk of rebirth, the suffering Lowry depicts in the novella remains that of the damned rather than those in the process of being redeemed. Only from the standpoint of the Nirvana principle does Plantagenet's symbolic return to the womb represent a triumph. One almost expects to come across a sign in Lowry's New York that reads *A Parián,* for *Lunar Caustic* clearly points the way to the Mexican Inferno. Nowhere is the affinity between the novella and *Under the Volcano* more marked than in the texture of the protagonists' consciousness. The passage in which Plantagenet's agony is compared to "a great lidless eye," for instance, contains unmistakably the germ of a Consular meditation: "The stars taking their places were wounds opening in his being, multiple duplications of that agony, of that eye. The constellations might have been monstrosities in the delirium of God. Disaster seemed smeared over the whole universe. It was as if he were living in the preexistence of some unimaginable catastrophe, and he steadied himself a moment against the sill, feeling the doomed earth itself stagger in its heaving spastic flight towards the Hercules Butterfly" (P267). One discovers an echo in Geoffrey Firmin's apocalyptic musing that "the earth was a ship, lashed by the Horn's tail, doomed never to make her Valparaiso. Or that it was like a golf ball, launched at Hercules' Butterfly, wildly hooked by a giant out of an asylum window in hell" (V287). The witty unfolding of metaphor in the latter quotation illustrates the gain in stylistic power that helps to distinguish the *Volcano* from the more discursive earlier work.

Pressed to provide a sequel to his chef d'oeuvre, Lowry commended *Lunar Caustic* to his editor as "a masterwork, or a potential one."[41] Few readers are likely to second this judgment. As it stands, the novella suffers from such serious defects as the obscurity of its protagonist's motivation, the flatness of its secondary characters, and the ponderousness of much of its symbolism. Lowry might have corrected at least some of these flaws had he been able to devote the six months of additional work to *Lunar Caustic* that would, he claimed, have sufficed to put it in its proper form. It is difficult to resist the conclusion, though, that the novella was never itself a masterpiece-in-embryo but that, like *Ultramarine,* its importance lies in its having prepared the artist to write *Under the Volcano.*

In the same year that he finished the initial version of *Lunar Caustic,* Lowry left New York for Los Angeles, where he evidently hoped to find work as a screenwriter. His Consul compares the "rending tumult" of these cities to the unbandaging of giants. The novelist and his heroes alike remind one of Baudelaire's "matelot ivrogne, inventeur d'Amériques / Dont l'image rend le gouffre plus amer."[42] Lowry remained in California for only a few months and then, with Jan, took ship for Mexico, sailing into Acapulco harbor on the Day of the Dead 1936.[43] "Like Columbus I have torn through one reality and discovered another," declared the artist the following year. "Alas, my only friend is the Virgin for those who have nobody with, and she is not much help, while I am on this last tooloose-Lowrytrek."[44] It was by no means the last of Lowry's perilous voyages, but it was undoubtedly the most decisive, as crucial for him as the journey up the Congo had been for Conrad.

2
Under the Volcano

A Book
of the Dead

There may be in the cup
A spider steeped and one may drink, depart,
And yet partake no venom, for his knowledge
Is not infected. But if one present
The abhorred ingredient to his eye, make known
How he hath drunk, he cracks his gorge, his sides,
With violent hefts. I have drunk, and seen the spider.
—Shakespeare, *The Winter's Tale*

La violence du venim tord mes membres, me rend
difforme, me terrasse. Je meurs de soif, j'étouffe,
je ne puis crier.... Un homme qui veut se mutiler
est bien damné, n'est-ce pas? Je me crois en enfer,
donc j'y suis.
—Rimbaud, *Une saison en enfer*

Lowry cast much of *Under the Volcano* in an apocalyptic-symbolist mode that springs from a correspondence between the "subnormal world" without and the "abnormally suspicious delirious one within him."[1] In order to grasp the reticulation of signs, portents, and motifs one should, the author insisted, read or, better, reread his book, bearing in mind "the poetical conception of the *whole*."[2] That the reader must bring to any given passage an awareness of the pertinent cross-references—its "spatial" design[3]—does not mean, however, that he should regard the book solely in this fashion. One may indeed apprehend a particular segment of Lowry's multilaminate prose in a single moment, but he should remember that each of these elements attains its full significance only as part of a dramatic development. Accordingly, we shall examine the chapters of Lowry's novel in the sequence he ordained. Any drastic rearrangement of the material would not only compromise its effectiveness, he rightly contended, but would also "buckle the very form of the book,...a wheel with twelve spokes, the motion of which is something like that...of time itself."[4]

A Virgil posing as Baedeker leads us into the Mexican *Inferno*. "Two mountain chains traverse the Republic roughly from north to south" (V3), our guide notes and then goes on to offer a matter-of-fact account of the situation and topography of Quauhnahuac, together with information about roads, hotels, places of worship, and recreational facilities likely to be of interest to the tourist. On a first reading one might find such items as the ratio of cantinas to churches curious: only when he returns to this chapter, which serves as both overture and coda, will these particulars gain their proper resonance. Apart from the title of the book and the fact that two volcanoes are said to dominate the valley, there is nothing to suggest the wealth of symbolic meaning that will attach itself to these peaks. Indeed Popocatepetl and Ixtaccihuatl are not even identified for several pages. Similarly, the observation that Quauhnahuac lies on the same parallel as Juggernaut signifies little until we learn that, like the god from whom the town in India takes its name, the old Aztec city has fed on terrible sacrifices. The traveler enters Quauhnahuac, we are told, via a highway that rapidly dissolves into "tortuous and broken" lanes and ends as a goat track. These details prefigure the labyrinthine story about to unfold, the tragedy or "goat-song" of a cuckold, a *cabrón*.[5]

Lowry attached special importance to his mise en scène: the initial chapter sets "the slow melancholy tragic rhythm of Mexico," he declared, "and above all [it] establishes the *terrain*."[6] Having provided us with a panoramic view of Quauhnahuac and the surrounding countryside in his first two paragraphs, the author is ready in the third to bring his theme into sharper focus. A single task remains for the guide: to direct us to one of the "many splendid hotels" in town. The Hotel Casino de la Selva seems an odd choice, for its jai-alai courts are "grassgrown and deserted," the springboards of its pool "empty and mournful," and the gaming tables no longer in operation: "You may not even dice for drinks at the bar. The ghosts of ruined gamblers haunt it." On the hillside behind the Casino, processions of mourners, "visible only as the melancholy lights of their candles" (V4), descend from the cemeteries. We have been conducted into what is, for all its beauty, a wasteland where the presence of the dead is felt more keenly than that of the living.

The story opens on the Day of the Dead (All Souls' Day, 2 November) 1939, two months after the invasion of Poland, with reflections on an event that has taken place exactly one year earlier, an occurrence that "seemed already to belong in a different age. One would have thought the horrors of the present would have swallowed it up like a drop of water. It was not so. Though tragedy was in the process of becoming unreal and meaningless it seemed one was still permitted to remember the days when an individual life held some value and was not a mere misprint in a communiqué" (V5). The reader does not know yet what has happened, but plainly the novelist is preparing him to respond to the account of it with pity and terror.[7] As the preceding meditation indicates, he was acutely conscious of the problem a writer faces in establishing, rather than merely asserting, the tragic status of an action: "it seemed one was still permitted to remember." Tragedy remains a valid mode only if one admits a great deal of ironic qualification. The power and universality of the novel derive to a considerable extent from implicit parallels between the doom that overtakes the principal characters and the horrors of a world at war. Mexico, "pyre of Bierce and springboard of Hart Crane, the age-old arena of racial and political conflicts,"[8] forms a backdrop in every way appropriate to the recounting of psychic battles.

No great distance separates the Casino de la Selva from the *selva oscura* in which Dante found himself, and indeed one of the two men seated on the hotel terrace, Jacques Laruelle, is in a quandary that recalls the Florentine's. Of this midlife crisis A. Alvarez observes: "The optimism and idealism of youth fall away before a more somber, less hopeful sense of the world as it is, unredeemed, uneasy, unforgiving. And in the warren of this depression all [one's] past work seems trivial or worthless, and [one's] internal resources hopelessly inadequate for the dour task of finding a way through in some new, untested direction. It is a despair not many steps from suicide."[9] Alvarez's remarks on the predicament of Dante apply not just to Jacques but to all the major characters in the novel. Unfortunately no Virgil is at hand to help Laruelle and the Firmins negotiate the dark wood. A pale surrogate, the kindly Dr. Vigil, directs them to a church for the bereaved, but his guidance proves ineffectual.

Clearly we are bound for regions where the clipped prose of a Baedeker will not serve. After the first few paragraphs, Lowry eases into a much more sensitive point of view, Laruelle's, and remains there for the rest of chapter 1. The conceits Jacques employs in an effort to make sense of the events he has experienced reveal his cast of mind: "He watched the clouds; dark swift horses surging up the sky. A black storm breaking out of its season! That was what love was like, he thought; love which came too late. . . . And let such love strike you dumb, blind, mad, dead— your fate would not be altered by your simile" (V10). In a manner characteristic of Lowry, this passage has a double reference. Its immediate relevance is to Jacques's illicit feelings for Yvonne, but it bears too on the Firmins' abortive marriage. Apocalyptic horses, emblematic of passions turned destructive, figure prominently in the *Volcano*. Laruelle cannot but have in mind the charging stallion, released by the Consul, which tramples Yvonne, although the reader will not recognize the allusion until he reaches the final chapters. One will surely find himself more profoundly affected on a second reading by the Frenchman's poignant realization that words offer scant relief from the exigencies of a tempestuous and hopeless love.

Laruelle encounters acute difficulty in distinguishing the real from the apparent among his tangled recollections, the rhythm of his involved thought finding an echo in the intricacy of Lowry's style.[10] As Jacques walks through the ruins of Miramar, the palace of Maximilian and Carlotta, he reflects: "And yet, how they must have loved this land, these two lonely empurpled exiles, human beings finally, lovers out of their element—their Eden, without either knowing quite why, beginning to turn under their noses into a prison and smell like a brewery, their only majesty at last that of tragedy" (V14). In his imagination Jacques listens to these ghosts, ruined gamblers whose paradise has become a place of confinement, carry on an impassioned dialogue; however, it is not Hapsburg voices he hears but those of Yvonne and Geoffrey. Every place he goes in Quauhnahuac is haunted by the memory of these two people he has loved and who are now, the reader infers from the elegiac tone of these remembrances, dead.

In the initial portion of the novel, our sympathy for the Consul stems in large part from Laruelle's identification with him. From the time of their first meeting in Courselles almost thirty years before, Geoffrey has influenced his friend in everything from his style of dress to his vocation as a filmmaker. One may even regard Jacques's liaison with Yvonne as the ultimate tribute to Geoffrey's taste; it constitutes perhaps the nearest approach the two men can make to a consummation of their relationship, short of an outright homosexual bond.[11] We learn subsequently that the Consul has virtually duped Laruelle into betraying him. In the aftermath of the murder in Parián, the Frenchman comes more and more to resemble his alter ego. He replaces the Consul as a substitute father to Hugh, and during the year that follows the catastrophe, he takes increasingly to drink in an effort to slake his thwarted craving for love.

Most decisive in shaping our attitude toward the protagonist are the tenderness with which Jacques recalls the youthful Geoffrey, a shy Anglo-Indian orphan trying desperately to emulate the "erect manly carriage" of the Taskersons, and the ardor with which he defends the war record of his friend, a naval officer decorated for his gallantry in vanquishing a German U-boat. This knowledge that the Consul was, at one point, a man of action does much to account for Laruelle's faith that "he might have actually proved a great force for good" (V31), and it significantly enhances his potentiality as a tragic character. Jacques's testimony to his friend's merits is especially moving when one considers the two men's estrangement from each other during the last months of Geoffrey's life and the apathy into which Laruelle himself has fallen, the abandonment of whatever hopes he had of changing the world through his art. A phrase Lowry employs to set the scene for these disclosures also describes aptly the tone of the narrative at this stage, one of pervasive gloom, as well as its impressionistic mode of sporadic but intense illuminations: we find ourselves peering into "a graveyard darkness, stabbed by flashes of torchlight like heat lightning" (V28).

There is no clearer indication of the extent to which Jacques has assumed his dead friend's identity than his playing the "absurd game" that had so delighted the Consul: "sortes Shakespeareanae." Opening Geoffrey's anthology of Elizabethan drama at random, his eye falls on lines "that seemed to have the power of carrying his...mind downward into a gulf, as in fulfilment on his own spirit of the threat Marlowe's Faustus had cast at his despair":

> *Then will I headlong fly into the earth:*
> *Earth, gape! it will not harbour me!* (V34)

The coincidence is of the fateful sort one expects to find in a Hardy novel; the reader discovers subsequently, however, that the occurrence is not so improbable after all. He learns that the Consul has been gathering material for a study concerning, among other things, "the cohabations of Faust" and that he is eager to retrieve the volume of plays he has lent Jacques. We may suppose that Geoffrey has turned to the passage in question on more than one occasion. In any case, the meaning of the coincidence deepens when Laruelle realizes that he has misread the text slightly: "Faustus had said: 'Then will I headlong run into the earth,' and 'Oh, no, it will not—' That was not so bad. Under the circumstances to run was not so bad as to fly" (V34). *Whose* circumstances? Is the Frenchman thinking of Faustus's thrust toward oblivion, Geoffrey's plunge into the abyss, or his own more gradual deterioration? Evidently the three have become all but indistinguishable. The minds of Lowry's characters are in large measure constitutive of what they perceive, and the more trying the conditions in which they find themselves, the more difficult it is to separate subject and object, self and other. In few novels is the reader precipitated into an epistemological thicket denser than the one confronting him in the *Volcano*.

Laruelle's game ends with his discovery of what may be described, in Joyce's phrase, as a "letter selfpenned to one's other."[12] Its opening lines underscore the Faustian character of the Consul: "Night: and once again, the nightly grapple with death, the room shaking with daemonic orchestras, the snatches of fearful sleep, the voices outside the window, my name being continually repeated with scorn by imaginary parties arriving, the dark's spinets" (V35). One can scarcely exaggerate the importance of this letter, which allows the reader to enter Geoffrey's consciousness for the first time, the only such access he is to have apart from the twelve hours during which the main action of the novel transpires. This interior view enables us to gauge the Consul's despair, at bottom a sense that he is radically unworthy to exist, as well as the rich possibilities open to him were he to regain his faith in life. As it is, he looks forward to a dawn without promise, except for that "cold jonquil beauty one rediscovers in death" (V35). The news that Yvonne has divorced him induces an odd feeling of "something like peace," as though his soul had indeed died.

Marlovian as Geoffrey's conception of his fate appears, there is another side of him that approaches the redemptive spirit of

Goethe.[13] As he composes his letter, he imagines an Edenic alternative to the hell that his mind, very much its own place, has made of Mexico: "I seem to see now, between mescals, this path, and beyond it strange vistas, like visions of a new life together we might somewhere lead. I seem to see us living in some northern country, of mountains and hills and blue water; our house is built on an inlet and one evening we are standing, happy in one another, on the balcony of this house, looking over the water" (V36-37). There follows a sublime, page-long evocation of this "strange vista," which turns out to be the spot known in all Lowry's fiction from the *Volcano* on as Eridanus, a tiny gathering of squatters' shacks on the foreshore of Burrard Inlet near Vancouver. The wonder of Geoffrey's vision resides not in its source, since he has been to British Columbia and even owns an island there, but in the possibility of renewed innocence.

Against the yearning to regain a paradise of salving love stands the Consul's urge to use his great mental powers to destroy himself. On the axis of these contending forces—hope and despair, salvation and doom, Eros and Thanatos—the action of the *Volcano* turns. Unfortunately the protagonist's dialectical balancing, his "teetering over the awful unbridgeable void" (V39), ends in paralysis rather than the equilibrium he seeks to maintain. The knowledge of a path through the Inferno Geoffrey attributes to Blake, reconciler of antinomies, whose imaginative reach he at moments rivals but whose grasp—the will to act on his perception—he lacks. He recognizes that without Yvonne's love he must perish and that he has only to summon her to assure her return. "But this is what it is to live in hell," he reflects. "I could not, cannot ask you" (V38). When the Consul's defenses crumble and he finally does plead with her to come back, "if only for a day" (V41), we know that his crippling ambivalence will render the cry futile. The letter to Yvonne remains unposted; indeed Geoffrey is conscious even as he writes it that it will never be sent. Perhaps because of this awareness, he expresses himself with a clarity and depth of feeling seldom equaled when his former wife actually does, on her own initiative, rejoin him. On that day, six months after his composition of the letter, the options threatening the redoubt of his isolation make this sort of honesty extraordinarily complicated.

The Consul's vision of a northern Eden breaks off when he perceives the wash from an "unseen ship, like a great wheel, the vast spokes of the wheel whirling across the bay—" (V38). This image prefigures the "luminous wheel" revolving at the close of chapter 1. Both the ship's wake and the Ferris wheel represent those awesome forces that catch men up and ferry them from one realm to another—from Quauhnahuac to Eridanus, from death to rebirth—in an unending cycle. The longing for paradise is itself inherently circular, for it entails the recovery of a happiness that has been lost. As Lowry explained to his publisher, the Ferris wheel points to eternal recurrence, the Buddhist conception of the law, and the very circumflexion of the narrative. "In an obvious movie sense," he observed, it is "the wheel of time whirling backwards until we have reached the year before and Chapter II." Its dynamics resemble those of a reel in one of Jacques's pictures, and "if we like, we can look at the rest of the book through Laruelle's eyes, as if it were his creation."[14] From this point of view, *Under the Volcano* becomes an oblique fulfillment of Jacques's wish to direct a Faust film.

The letter in which Geoffrey envisions his Eden is written, appropriately enough, on Hotel Bella Vista stationery, and it is there, in the Bella Vista bar, that Yvonne discovers him upon her return to Quauhnahuac. As an alternative to the fatal course he has been pursuing, she offers him the rebirth of love amid a crystal forest of which he has dreamed. Lowry renders her first sight of the Consul in a passage that juxtaposes the freedom and vitality of the sea[15] with the close, almost suffocating, atmosphere of the bar: fresh from her voyage down the coast, Yvonne enters

> silently, blinking, myopic in the swift leathery perfumed
> alcoholic dusk, the sea that morning going in with her, rough

and pure, the long dawn rollers advancing, rising, and
crashing down to glide, sinking, in colourless ellipses over
the sand. . . .
   The bar was empty, however.
   Or rather it contained one figure. . . . Yvonne felt her spirit
that had flown to meet this man's as if already sticking to the
leather. (V45–46)

The image of "dawn rollers," associated with the hopes that have
accompanied Yvonne to Mexico and indicative, once again, of
things turning back upon themselves, recurs in chapter 11 as she
lies beneath the rearing horse. There the accent falls heavily on
"sinking," on the collapse of her dream. That failure is adum-
brated here in chapter 2 by her "myopic" inability to coordinate
her vision of the world with Geoffrey's.

   Yvonne has resolved to share his life, to drink along with him if
necessary, but she is constitutionally incapable of doing so. To
her the murkiness of the bar signifies the annihilation of their
love. She cannot comprehend that, for the Consul, "it is not altogether darkness." As her eyes follow his about the bar, he tries,
silently, to communicate the maze of emotions such places arouse
in him: "not even the gates of heaven, opening wide to receive
me, could fill me with such celestial complicated and hopeless joy
as the iron screen that rolls up with a crash, as the unpadlocked
jostling jalousies which admit those whose souls tremble with the
drinks they carry unsteadily to their lips. All mystery, all hope, all
disappointment, yes, all disaster, is here, beyond those swinging
doors" (V50). Insofar as Yvonne becomes aware of these sentiments, they cannot but strike her as the height of oxymoronic
perversity. It would appear, however, that she apprehends very
little of what Geoffrey seeks to transmit.[16] Even the simplest facts
of his cosmos remain for her obscure. The confusion she experiences in determining how many people there are in the Bella Vista
bar underscores her perceptual limitations. Initially she hesitates
to go in because the sound of voices leads her to imagine the room
crowded. When she does enter, the bar seems vacant, until finally

her eyes adjust to the gloom and she discerns her former husband. Several minutes elapse before, prompted by the Consul's glance, she remarks the presence of another person, an old woman sitting in the corner. "How unless you drink as I do," his love asks her, "can you hope to understand the beauty of an old woman from Tarasço, who plays dominoes at seven o'clock in the morning?" (V50) But the sight of this ancient crone, a representative of Geoffrey's—and her own—fatality, petrifies Yvonne.

The heroine's difficulties in attuning herself to an alien realm seem minor when one compares the rents in her former husband's relations with his world and with himself. At times he does attain an odd kind of balance, the "complicated...joy" mentioned above, but it is exceedingly volatile. The disposition of nature and consciousness first to mirror each other and then, abruptly, to disjoin causes the protagonist to feel metaphysically outcast. In a moment of silence that punctuates an attempt by Geoffrey and Yvonne to revive their former intimacy, he listens to water trickling into a swimming pool:

> There was something else; the Consul imagined he still heard the music of the ball, which must have long since ceased, so that this silence was pervaded as with a stale thudding of drums. Pariah: that meant drums too. Parián. It was doubtless the almost tactile absence of the music however, that made it so peculiar the trees should be apparently shaking to it, an illusion investing not only the garden but the plains beyond, the whole scene before his eyes, with horror, the horror of an intolerable unreality. This must be not unlike, he told himself, what some insane person suffers at those moments when, sitting benignly in the asylum grounds, madness suddenly ceases to be a refuge and becomes incarnate in the shattering sky. (V75)

It appears that in Parián, in the Farolito, the Consul may be able to keep the drumming of his pariah soul in time with the daemonic orchestration of the spheres; even there, however, the relief he obtains through drink transforms itself without warning into nightmares. Only through the legerdemain of style—the "palliative of articulate art," as Nabokov has it—can one hope to arrange these dissonances into an enduring harmony. Unfortunately Geoffrey remains a blocked poet, although he realizes that "it is perhaps a good idea under the circumstances to pretend at least to be proceeding with one's great work" (V39).

The Consul is forced to recognize that the cosmos does not invariably respond to his projection of himself, that it is in fact radically *other:* "The sun shining brilliantly now on all the world before him, its rays picking out the timberline of Popocatepetl as its summit like a gigantic surfacing whale shouldered out of the clouds again, all this could not lift his spirit. The sunlight could not share his burden of conscience, of sourceless sorrow. It did not know him" (V76). So grave is Geoffrey's sense of dispossession that it seems to place his very being in jeopardy. A man suffering from acute ontological insecurity exists, remarks R. D. Laing, "under the black sun, the evil eye, of his own scrutiny."[17] Withering self-awareness of this sort calls to mind Ahab, meditating upon the setting sun; "This lovely light, it lights not me; ...damned, most subtly and most malignantly! damned in the midst of Paradise!"[18] Their feelings of estrangement lead both Ahab and Geoffrey to perform cabalistic exercises, efforts to dominate the phenomenal world by arranging it into arcane patterns of correspondence. Behind these attempts lies the desire of each man to captain his own fate. In an earlier version of the *Volcano,* Lowry explicitly likens the snow-capped Popocatepetl to Moby Dick.[19] The simile is apt, for the mountain and the whale both serve as titular symbols, all-encompassing repositories of meaning, whether intrinsic or imposed.

Just how difficult it is for Geoffrey to orient himself becomes evident when he collapses in the street, the fall being less significant than his inverted perception of it: "suddenly the Calle Nicaragua rose up to meet him" (V77). The Consul knows very well that he is engineering his own destruction. Sprawled on the road, he imagines that Hugh has come to lend him a hand and discourses on the younger man's affair with Yvonne. Lest remorse overtake Hugh on this account, Geoffrey seeks to placate his brother's conscience: "Does this help, what I am trying to tell you, that *I* realize to what degree I brought all this upon myself?" (V79). The overture is as much an effort to suture together the Consul's own wounds as it is an attempt to heal the breach between the two men. It can hardly accomplish the latter, since the admission is not made in Hugh's actual presence. Geoffrey's words do, however, dispose the reader to see him as more than a pawn of the historical forces reflected in the events of his last day. He selects the course he will follow and, regardless of the factors that condition his choice, he accepts responsibility for it. This affirmation confers upon the Consul a measure of Ahabian dignity.

Of his wife Ahab confesses: "I widowed that poor girl when I married her."[20] The Firmins' divorce presents itself in an analogous fashion: both partners experience the rupture as a proximate form of death. During the year of Yvonne's absence Geoffrey has suffered "such desolation, such a desperate sense of abandonment, bereavement, as . . . he had never known in his life, unless it was when his mother died" (V197–98). Yet the longed-for moment of reunion awakens all the Consul's old ambivalence; his former wife's gestures evoke, on the one hand, "the whole queer secret dumbshow of incommunicable tendernesses and loyalties and eternal hopes of their marriage" and, on the other, "a sense, almost, of indecency that he, a stranger, should be in her room" (V87). It becomes plain that his apprehension of himself as an intruder in her bedchamber is not a consequence of their divorce but one of the grounds for it. Yvonne, whose beauty is at once "youthful and ageless," calls forth Geoffrey's idealized recollection of his mother so strongly that he refuses, unconsciously, to sully the imago. Her liaisons with Hugh and Jacques compound the problem, for they cannot but strike him as tantamount to incest.

Given the oedipal strain in the Firmins' relationship, one is scarcely surprised to find that they have great difficulty in consummating it. Geoffrey appears a singularly half-hearted lover as he plays "the prelude, the preparatory nostalgic phrases on his wife's senses, . . . the little one-fingered introduction to the unclassifiable composition that might still just follow" (V89–90). The tenuous endeavor to compose at least a moment of erotic harmony fails, just as the Consul's struggle to penetrate the cosmic mysteries has been thwarted. In terms of the protagonist's cabalistic pursuits, concord between man and wife and the mystic's fidelity to his calling amount to the same thing.[21] Even as he attempts the sexual prelude, Geoffrey compares it to "that jewelled gate the desperate neophyte, Yesod-bound, projects for the thousandth time on the heavens to permit passage of his astral body" (V89).

Those readers who prefer to attribute the Consul's impotence to excessive drinking rather than psychical conflict will have a hard time accounting for his effective performance with María in the Farolito.[22] In one sense, of course, the failure does stem from his dipsomania; the cantinas have become a perverse substitute for both marital felicity and mystical union.[23] The voice of one of Geoffrey's familiar spirits, speaking on behalf of Yvonne and of his own repressed longings, declares: "All your love is in the cantinas now: the feeble survival of a love of life now turned to poison, . . . and poison has become your daily food" (V65). While he is trying to make love, an insistent refrain reminiscent of Yeats's "Lake Isle of Innisfree" enters his thoughts; incapable of rising to the occasion, "now, now he wanted to go." And the image of a heavenly portal yields to that of El Puerto del Sol, a "gate" that is not at all strait, where the sunlight descends "in a single golden line as if in the act of conceiving a God, falling like a lance straight into a block of ice—" (V90). This gelid theogony foreshadows the dreadful issue of Geoffrey's copulation with the prostitute in chapter 12. Indeed the entire scene involving María ironically counterpoints the frustration of those "eternal hopes" rekindled by Yvonne's return.

But the tension persists: even after his confession of impotence the protagonist refuses to make a clear-cut decision in favor of drink. Instead he pours himself two glasses, one of whiskey and the other of the supposedly therapeutic strychnine mixture Hugh · has been urging on him, and wryly compares their value as aphrodisiacs. "Perhaps it will take immediate effect. It still may not be too late," he reflects, looking at the strychnine. "One must never forget either that alcohol is a food. How can a man be expected to perform his marital duties without food? Marital? At all events I am progressing, slowly but surely" (V90–92). Geoffrey's progress, which is anything but irreversible, consists in his remaining at home rather than fleeing to a bar. "What am I talking about?" he interrupts his thoughts to ask. "Even I know I am being fatuous" (V92). He foresees clearly enough the end to which his internal contradictions are leading: the vision of a dead man, the "other," beside the pool is a recurrent one, adumbrating not only the moribund Indian in chapter 8 but his own death as well. The vultures that hover above the Consul, their "soft hoarse cries like the cries of love" (V147), reinforce the sense of impending doom.

Under the Volcano seems, by the end of the third chapter, to be sinking ever more deeply into the action of a mind that renders even the most common occurrences rich and strange. Chapter 4, Hugh and Yvonne's horseback ride, varies the pace of Lowry's narrative; stylistically, it offers relief from Geoffrey's tortuous monologues and, thematically, a breath of hope. If the Consul has shown himself to be a dubious Faust during his *Stündchen* with Yvonne, then she has been a rather frigid Gretchen. In Hugh's eyes, though, she represents still the *Ewig-Weibliche,* "clothed entirely in sunlight" (V95) and capable of drawing a man out of himself.[24] The drift toward death appears to be suspended through most of chapter 4, and a "little world of love" begins to blossom. Unfortunately the Consul's wife and brother cannot enjoy it with a clear conscience; a billy goat, a *cabrón,* the emblem of Geoffrey's cuckoldry, observes their progress. Since Hugh and Yvonne have both come to Quauhnahuac hoping to salvage him, any attempt to resume their liaison would constitute an insupportable breach of faith. Remorse for their previous lapse weighs upon them already. Furthermore, whatever joy Hugh experiences seems to him to have been purchased at the expense of his comrades in Spain, who are losing the battle for Catalonia while he idles in the sun. The two strands of guilt intertwine when he reflects: "By some contrariety we have been allowed for one hour a glimpse of what never was at all, of what never can be since brotherhood was betrayed, the image of our happiness" (V107). Hugh's passionate longing "to be, to do, good" (V124) may be quixotic, but even if that is so, he resembles the Don less in his laughable aspect than in his tragic one.

Yvonne returns to Geoffrey with the explicit intention of offering him the fresh start they both crave and an intimation that Canada may be the place to essay it. When she raises the question with Hugh, who serves as his brother's activist alter ego, the project seems to him "the best and easiest and most simple thing in the world" (V121). It is he who proposes that they settle on an inlet of the sea, remote from civilized cares:

No phone, No rent, No consulate. Be a squatter. Call on your pioneer ancestors. Water from the well. Chop your own wood. After all, Geoff's as strong as a horse. And perhaps he'll be able really to get down to his book and you can have your stars and the sense of the seasons again; though you can sometimes swim late as November. And get to know the real people: the seine fishermen, the old boatbuilders, the trappers, . . . the last truly free people left in the world. (V122)

Hugh's idiom takes its coloration from his cowboy-revolutionary swagger; nonetheless, even the bromides about "pioneer ancestors" and "real people" help establish the moral magnetism of the Eridanus theme. Yvonne takes his remarks about the virtues of self-reliance and aligning oneself with the fundamental rhythms of nature as compass points in her subsequent reveries concerning the pier they would build with their own hands and the swims, Thoreauvian rites of purification, they would enjoy in the cold sea. The Consul's long-deferred study of arcane wisdom might still be written—and tragedy averted—if he could somehow manage to graft his seasoned intellect onto the young man's vitality Hugh embodies.[25]

The salvation that appears so simple to Hugh is, in Geoffrey's eyes, "large with menace" (V83). Paradise regained in no way precludes the possibility of a second expulsion more rending than the first. In any case, the protagonist remains uncertain that Eden would constitute an agreeable habitat. Bunyan's words, in the epigraph drawn from *Grace Abounding,* are apposite: "I could not find with all my soul that I did desire deliverance." In chapter 5 the Consul goes so far as to speculate that Adam might not have been exiled from the garden at all: "What if his punishment really consisted . . . in his having to *go on living there,* alone, of course—suffering, unseen, cut off from God" (V133). And indeed the land in which the narrative is set evinces still, despite the rank and gross elements that possess it, "the beauty of the Earthly Paradise" (V10). The author himself regarded the Eden motif—"Le gusta este jardín?"—as the most important in the novel.[26]

Firmin's encounter with Mr. Quincey over the fence that divides his own unweeded garden from his neighbor's fastidiously tended one provides an occasion for some of Lowry's most antic wit. When Geoffrey learns, for instance, that his brother and rival in love has returned to the house and departed again, accompanied by Yvonne, he seeks to distract himself in the following manner:

> "—Hullo-hullo-look-who-comes-hullo-my-little-snake-in-the-grass-my-little-anguish-in-herba—" the Consul at this moment greeted Mr. Quincey's cat, . . . "hello-pussy-my-little-Priapusspuss, my-little-Oedipusspusspuss," and the cat, recognizing a friend and uttering a cry of pleasure,

wound through the fence and rubbed against the Consul's legs, purring. "My little Xicotancatl." The Consul stood up. He gave two short whistles while below the cat's ears twirled. "She thinks I'm a tree with a bird in it," he added.

"I wouldn't wonder," retorted Mr. Quincey. (V134-35)

Geoffrey's humor is not entirely whimsical. He addresses Hugh, when the latter returns, as an "old snake in the grass" (V141), one whose Priapean leanings might transform the Edenic "splendor in the grass," as Wordsworth has it, into sorrow. Xicontancatl's hidden treasure threatens at any moment to turn into Oedipus's terrible secret and the Consul's katabasis into "cat abysses" (V136). Geoffrey does in fact imagine himself being drawn on past some larger felids, the "wandering dreaming lions" that stalk the Parián wilderness, "towards ineluctable personal disaster, always in a delightful way of course; the disaster might even be found at the end to contain a certain element of triumph" (V139). An allegory of imminent catastrophe and miraculous redemption enacts itself before his eyes when Quincey's cat traps a butterfly. Just as the animal extends a paw for the kill, the insect, whose luminous wings have never ceased beating, makes good its escape, "as might indeed the human soul from the jaws of death" (V140). Geoffrey, an adept "catastrophysicist," has no difficulty in reading the significance of these events. The little "popocat" comes to seem nearly as laden with portentous meaning as the volcano itself. Wit of the felicitous sort Lowry weaves around the cat derives not directly from Joyce, as some readers have supposed, but from another master of the double entendre, Aiken.[27] All three are, of course, drinking writers with a keen sense of how one exploits the artistic possibilities of *Katzenjammer.*

As the fractured quotation from Dante at the beginning of chapter 6 implies, Hugh's raison d'être has become almost as obscure as the Consul's: "Nel mezzo del bloody cammin di nostra vita mi ritrovai in. . . ." (V150). The young man's wish to find his

43

proper identity by performing sacrificial deeds is frustrated when all his feats turn out to be self-serving. In a half-comical attempt to isolate a disinterested act, he recalls aiding a seagull, but the bird, unlike Bloom's gull in "Circe," refuses to testify on his behalf; his charity has been tainted by his dramatizing of it. Hugh is forced to recognize that he is no Saint Julian but rather a jongleur, a mock-chivalric pursuer of married women who dreams "of dying, bitten by lions, in the desert, at the last calling for [his] guitar, strumming to the end" (V178). At no point does Hugh seem more akin to his brother than when he contemplates his own immolation. The self-deprecating humor, the ironic gaiety, with which both characters confront that eventuality allows the reader to judge them much more sympathetically than he otherwise might.[28] Toward the close of chapter 6, the three Firmins depart for the *corrida* in Tomalín. Only the Consul foresees with any clarity their ultimate destination; Hugh senses, however, as they set off in the opposite direction from his ride with Yvonne, that the hopes of that idyllic hour are already as remote as childhood.

For Lowry the believer in hermetic correspondences—"Boehme would support me," he declared, "when I speak of the passion for order even in the smallest things"[29]—the number seven was steeped in fatality. It conveys, like the angel that issues forth when the seventh seal is opened, the following message: "Woe, woe, woe, to the inhabiters of the earth" (Revelation 8:13). At seven in the evening Geoffrey frees the horse with the figure seven branded on its rump, an act that precipitates his own and Yvonne's deaths and her subsequent translation to the Pleiades, which represent the celestial obverse of the fateful number. And it is chapter 7, the navel of the book, that poses most acutely several questions upon which the Consul's life direction hinges. Perhaps the most crucial of these is: "Could one be faithful to Yvonne and the Farolito both?" (V201). The all too manifest answer is no. Geoffrey cares for Yvonne but the cantinas still more; it is the Farolito to which he is now wedded: "his soul was locked with the essence of the place . . . and he was gripped by thoughts like those of the mariner who, sighting the faint beacon of Start Point after a long voyage, knows that soon he will embrace his wife" (V201). Distinct as this preference is, the grounds for it are not, and they bear looking into.

The Consul's ambivalence toward Yvonne, the tenderness he continues to feel for her versus the inability to pardon her trespasses, stems from his ties to his mother, whose ghost returns not just on All Souls' Day but throughout his life. That she should have died while he was still a small boy, thwarting his oedipal aspirations in the most decisive way possible, strikes him as an intolerable lapse. He cannot, on the deepest stratum of his nature, forgive this abandonment, and he visits vengeance for it on all the mother figures he subsequently encounters, beginning with his father's second wife. Thus he identifies with the dead child of Yvonne's previous marriage and imagines himself as "innocent as that other Geoffrey had been, who sat as in an organ loft somewhere playing, pulling out all the stops at random, and kingdoms divided and fell, and abominations dropped from the sky" (V146). The Consul's plight has been exacerbated by his father's mysterious disappearance in the Himalayas. Laruelle recalls the adolescent Geoffrey as a brooding, self-contained boy who sometimes burst into tears at the mention of the words "father" and "mother."

At forty-two the protagonist of the *Volcano* still feels himself to be very much an orphan, a stranger drifting through an inhospitable world. And with those who do proffer the love of which he was so early and cruelly deprived, the Consul wills exactly what he dreads most: the reenactment of his betrayal. It may be that he is compelled to repeat the traumatic experiences of childhood in the unconscious hope that by returning to the root of his predicament he might find a way of resolving it or at least of steeling himself to the pain it entails. Freud insisted that psychological disorders are in fact misguided attempts to surmount the impediments that have given rise to them. The effects of the Consul's urge to recapitulate his early abandonment are, of course, anything but life-enhancing; his compulsion appears rather to pertain to the death trend.[30]

One can unravel this paradoxical commingling of Eros and Thanatos most effectively by examining the reasons for Geoffrey's drinking. As we have observed in *Ultramarine* and *Lunar Caustic,* alcohol serves Lowry's protagonists as an ersatz for the maternal breast if not the womb. But with the Consul the longing goes even further back: he craves ultimately a reversion to the tranquility of the inorganic, the stony peace of the grave, which represents for him both a symbolic reunion with his lost parents and an actual one with the "elements" from which he has become estranged.[31] Hence the Farolito, where "life reached bottom," promises "an almost healing love" (V200). His drinking is a form of chronic suicide, a means of shortening the detour to death.

The character of Geoffrey's regressive tendency reveals itself clearly during his visit to the Terminal Cantina El Bosque. He associates the name with the dark forest passage in the *Inferno* that has played through Hugh's mind in the preceding chapter. The Consul introduces a slight variation: Dante's "selva oscura" becomes his "bosca oscura." Lest any doubt exist concerning the significance of the thicket, the voice of a familiar declares: "this is what it is like to die, just this and no more, an awakening from a dream in a dark place" (V226). Situated at the end of a bus line, the cantina prefigures a more extreme terminus. When Geoffrey speaks with the sympathetic proprietress, he thinks, for an instant, that he is "looking at his own mother. . . . He wanted to embrace Señora Gregorio, to cry like a child, to hide his face in her bosom" (V229). At the same time, she evokes, like other reflections of his mother, the bleakness of separation. Her bond with the Consul is one of "shared misery," since both have been abandoned by their spouses. Señora Gregorio, herself without a home, can do little to appease his longing for maternal solicitude; she has only tequila and the cover of her "shadow" to offer. Kindly as she is, the señora figures forth the devouring aspect of the mother archetype. She seems, in this respect, a sister to the old Tarascan woman we have seen in the Bella Vista and who appears once again in the Farolito.

Another key question raised in chapter 7 concerns the validity of Geoffrey's heroic aspirations: "You deny the greatness of my battle? Even if I win?" he asks Jacques, then adds, "And I shall certainly win, if I want to" (V219). That last claim, tinged with hubris, recalls his Faustian vaunt at the end of chapter 3: "The will of man is unconquerable. Even God cannot conquer it" (V93). The Consul appears to be fighting less to preserve human consciousness, as he maintains, than to transcend it; a latter-day incarnation of the Massachusetts settler William Blackstone,[32] he seeks not to vanquish the Indians who dwell within, on that "final frontier of consciousness" (V135) bordering the unconscious, but to cross over and join them. A heightened awareness of the energies they symbolize may be one of the Consul's objectives; he purchases this illumination, however, through a *dérèglement de tous les sens* that hastens the moment of final oblivion.

Laruelle argues that the baneful effects of Geoffrey's campaign far outweigh the gains, that the price he pays for intensity of perception is a narrowing of its scope. "Ben Jonson...or perhaps it was Christopher Marlowe, your Faust man, saw the Carthaginians fighting on his big toe-nail," remarks Jacques, by way of illustration. "That's like the kind of clear seeing you indulge in. Everything seems perfectly clear, because indeed it is perfectly clear, in terms of the toe-nail" (V217).[33] Both physiologically and morally alcohol does reduce one's peripheral vision, not to mention the distortions that occur in the center of the field, but if Laruelle supposes that a man can enjoy anything more than perspectives on the truth, there is nothing in the novel to support his contention. Lowry compensates for the limits that the personal equation imposes by having all the major characters present their points of view. More important still is the way he allows each of them and the Consul in particular to assess his own situation from different angles.

The altercation between Jacques and Geoffrey over the moral

standing of the latter's "great battle" concludes as follows: "You've even been insulated from the responsibility of genuine suffering. . . . Even the suffering you do endure is largely unnecessary. Actually spurious. It lacks the very basis you require of it for its tragic nature" (V219). These words appear to be spoken by Jacques, but it turns out that in the course of the argument he has slipped away and that the Consul has subsequently conducted both halves of the dialogue. Geoffrey's ability to play the roles of *alazon* and *eiron* at the same time would seem to disprove his friend's charge of purblindness, if Jacques is in fact the one who has framed the accusation, and tends to underscore the protagonist's heroic status. Yet in Lowry's world, experience has so many facets that qualifications are often doubled and redoubled. Shortly after his critical moment of self-recognition the Consul finds himself in the *máquina infernal* and reflects: "It was doubtless another example of Jacques'—Jacques?—unnecessary suffering" (V222). Firmin's repression of insights he has had into his predicament constitutes a form of tragic irony raised to the *n*th power.

For one who desires to fathom "secret knowledge" and, above all, the mystery of his own selfhood, the *máquina* incident poses questions of the highest importance. In an early draft of the *Volcano,* the Consul speculates: "Before you knew anything about life, you had the symbols. . . . Life was indeed what you made of the symbols and the less you made of life the more symbols you got."[34] In the course of revision, abstract discourse yielded to indirect methods of presentation and this passage dropped out. A trace of it survives, though, in Geoffrey's sense, as he tumbles in the *máquina infernal,* that "it was symbolic, of what he could not conceive, but it was undoubtedly symbolic" (V222). Even in context the antecedent of "it" remains unclear, an ambiguity that reflects the enigmatic character of his being-in-the-world. The loop-the-loop, which suggests "some huge evil spirit," is indeed the Consul's Sphinx, spinning out riddles of identity. Appropriately, the monster's name derives from *La machine infernale,*

Jean Cocteau's adaptation of the Oedipus myth.[35] Hanging in his cage, the Consul sees the world transposed, "with its people stretching out down to him, about to fall off the road onto his head, or into the sky. 999" (V222). The multitudes clinging to the road, the perilous *cammin di nostra vita*, represent a line of descent that, however alien it may seem to him, continues to fix the terms of his existence. This 999 is the 666 that recurs at so many points in the *Volcano* turned upside down, a variation on the Sphinx's riddle. The figure 666 is both "the number of a man" and of the apocalyptic beast (Revelation 13:18), the antagonist of "that poor fool who was bringing light to the world" (V222) and who was suspended above it for his pains.

Geoffrey experiences the whirling of the *máquina* as a "recessive unwinding." Artifacts that recall the roles thrust upon him are wrested from his pockets—an emptying out of self he finds more than welcome: "Let everything go! Everything particularly that provided means of ingress or egress, went bond for, gave meaning or character, or purpose or identity to that frightful bloody nightmare he was forced to carry around with him everywhere upon his back, that went by the name of Geoffrey Firmin" (V223). It is the nightmare of his personal and racial history from which the Consul, like Stephen Dedalus, wishes to awake. But no loop-the-loop machine can relieve him of that burden; the children who minutes before had tried unsuccessfully to beg coins from him restore his belongings. These children are themselves symbolic of a trust in life from which his past bars him. Geoffrey resembles the lame Indian at the end of chapter 9, a Mexican Aeneas who bears not only his father but the weight of an entire culture on his back.

The infernal machine stands as a symbol of those centrifugal forces that rend both psyche and society. Chapter 8 underscores the extent to which the Consul's isolation mirrors the disintegration around him with the journalistic clarity appropriate to an episode seen through Hugh's eyes. Indeed the narrative reaches beyond the insistent obviousness of the newspaper reporter to that of the homilist, as well it might, since its paradigm is Jesus' parable of the good Samaritan. "Christ, why can't we be simple," thinks Hugh, "why may we not all be brothers?" (V240). The culprit, it would seem, is the law.

In varying degrees, both Hugh and Geoffrey feel an obligation to treat the Indian agonizing by the roadside as their neighbor; however, as one of their fellow passengers on the Tomalín bus informs them, Mexican law forbids passersby to intervene in cases where foul play is suspected. The Consul, "the one among them most nearly representing authority" (V242), greets this reminder with relief and attempts to persuade his brother that the statute protects the victim. "Actually it's a sensible law," he adds. "Otherwise you might become an accessory after the fact" (V243). Geoffrey's reasoning can hardly salve either Hugh's conscience or his own. Plainly it is not the law of the land that constrains them but rather, as Saint Paul has it, the law in their members, the dictates of self-preservation and personal convenience. The other travelers join in the debate over what course to pursue, the mode of their deliberation resembling one of the Consul's alcoholic monologues—and arriving at the same point:

> One of them now should go for help, for the police. . . . But it was absurd to suppose the police were not on their way. How could the chingados be on their way when half of them were on strike? No it was only a quarter of them that were on strike. . . . Get Dr. Figueroa. Un hombre noble. But there was no phone. Oh, there was a phone once, in Tomalín, but it had decomposed. No, Doctor Figueroa had a nice new phone. Pedro, the son of Pepe, whose mother-in-law was Josefina, who also knew, it was said, Vicente González, had carried it through the streets himself. . . .
>
> There was no limit to their ingenuity. Though the most potent and final obstacle to doing anything about the Indian was this discovery that it wasn't one's own business, but someone else's. (V245)

The only person willing to become involved is a *pelado*, an heir to the conquistadores, who bases his action squarely on the law of self-interest; he steals what remains of the dying man's money and pays his fare with it.

Official codes have scant relevance in Parián state, for the right-wing dissidents from the Cárdenas government that dominate local affairs are among the least law-abiding elements in the society.[36] Three of these *sinarquistas* finally come upon the scene and take charge. That they are the very ones who attacked the Indian in the first place seems not unlikely. He appears to have been a courier for the Banco Ejidal, the agency responsible for implementing Cárdenas' agrarian reforms, and his waylayers might well have sought both the cash in his saddlebags and the liquidation of a political opponent. Or it may be that such conjectures are mistaken and that the victim is simply a peon whose horse has thrown him. Since the events leading up to the calamity and the vigilantes' subsequent interest in the case are both uncertain, it is easiest just to leave matters in their hands. The relationship of the Indian and his potential deliverers is analogous to that of Republican Spain and the Western democracies in the era of Munich.[37] Only Hugh, whose mind has been occupied all day with the Loyalist defeat on the Ebro, opposes the act of betrayal, and his resistance is quickly overcome. Geoffrey plays the role of Chamberlain, holding his brother on board the *camión* as it departs.

More exact parallels link the Indian's agony with the Consul's death in chapter 12. A sense of lost bearings pervades the two scenes. In the first Hugh compares this dislocation to Joshua's halting the sun, and in the second Geoffrey feels that "both his will, and time, . . . were paralysed" (V369). At moments the atmosphere of unreality seems almost playful. In chapter 8 Hugh and one of the deputies engage in a shoving match, during which the latter fumbles with his holster: "it was a manoeuvre, not to be taken seriously" (V247). After a similar scuffle outside the Farolito, his brother is equally unwilling to regard the Chief of Rostrums' pistol waving as a genuine threat: " 'No, I wouldn't do that,' said the Consul quietly, turning round. 'That's a Colt '17, isn't it? It throws a lot of steel shavings' " (V373). His tone parodies the white-hat bravado of Western films.[38] Unfortunately the Chief, who is acting in terms of another convention, misses his cue and pulls the trigger on his mocking adversary.

Geoffrey and the Indian are both, in one sense, political martyrs. Whatever doubt remains about the role of the Unión Militar in the Tomalín road slaying, it is clear that they share with the victim responsibility for the catastrophe in Parián.[39] In each case the onlookers respond to the dying man's plight with a mélange of sentiments ranging from scorn to compassion. *Pelados* are in attendance on both occasions, with the crucial difference that in the second scene Geoffrey has himself "become the pelado, the thief—yes, the pilferer of meaningless muddled ideas out of which his rejection of life had grown" (V374). *In extremis* the two unfortunates crave solidarity with their kind; the Indian's sole utterance is "Compañero," the word that gives solace to the Consul as life ebbs from him. The serpentine barranca that figures so prominently in the latter's end is present as well in chapter 8: "It appeared overtly horrendous here. In the bus one looked straight down, as from the maintruck of a sailing ship, through dense foliage and wide leaves that did not at all conceal the treachery of the drop. . . . Hugh saw a dead dog right at the bottom, nuzzling the refuse" (V233). The ravine corresponds to the fissures in man's nature that make living with himself and others such a complicated task, and it represents, ultimately, the metaphysical abyss that jeopardizes all values. The putrefying dog is a near relation of the one in El Bosque to which Geoffrey has made an appalling promise: "Yet this day, pichicho, shalt thou be with me in—" (V229).[40] And it foreshadows the pariah cur thrown after the Consul as a kind of viaticum at the close of chapter 12.

Throughout the novel the barranca remains unequivocally infernal, a "general Tartarus and gigantic jakes" (V131). One sees the volcanoes, however, from a variety of angles, indicative of the manifold significance they assume. "Ixtaccihuatl had side-slipped out of sight," observes the narrator, as the bus descends into Tomalín, "but...Popocatepetl slid in and out of view continually, never appearing the same twice,...incalculably distant at one moment, at the next looming round the corner with its splendid thickness of sloping fields, valleys, timber, its summit swept by clouds, slashed by hail and snow" (V252). These evershifting perspectives recall Proust's deployment of the spires of Combray in *Du côté de chez Swann.*

The Sierra Madre is frequently identified with the burden of memory. "From these mountains," remarks Laruelle, "emanated a strange melancholy force," emblematic of "the weight of many things, but mostly that of sorrow" (V13). Yvonne regards the volcanoes as "remote ambassadors of Mauna Loa, Mokuaweoweo" (V58), peaks she associates with her unhappy Hawaiian childhood, and for Geoffrey they are reminders of his early years in India and the loss of his parents. Popo and Ixta reflect not just the personal histories of these characters but also the tragic past of Mexico: they have witnessed conquests—Aztec, Spanish, French—brutal dictatorships, and civil strife that has resulted in such atrocities as women being crucified in the bull ring of Quauhnahuac.

But the volcanoes have another, more hopeful aspect as well. There may exist at the core of human nature a reserve of energy comparable to the "wild strength" of these mountains that will enable men to transcend their guilt-ridden pasts. "Old Popeye" may be "completely obliterated in spinach" (V75), but that does not mean that he cannot emerge again, perhaps more puissant than before. Like the comic-strip hero, the Consul flexes his biceps and concludes that he is "still strong as a horse" (V71). Geoffrey dreams, with "heaven aspiring" heart, of "the mighty mountain Himavat" (V125), and Hugh expresses a desire to climb Popocatepetl. In both instances one perceives a Faustian longing to surmount the despair that stems from earlier defeats. A voice instructs the Consul, as he writes his letter to Yvonne: "Lift up your eyes unto the hills" (V40). Salvation might indeed lie in that direction, the one from which his wife returns to him, for Popocatepetl and Ixtaccihuatl, the resting places of a fabled Aztec warrior and his princess, constitute an "image of the perfect marriage" (V93). When Yvonne comes back, she and Geoffrey do experience "a shared, a mountain peace," but it is unfortunately "a lie" (V64). In chapter 9 she observes Popo in her compact mirror and tries to fit Ixta in beside him; no matter how she turns the mirror, though, she cannot bring the two peaks within its compass.

Geoffrey's tendency to measure Yvonne against an imago finds a parallel in her attitude toward him. As she watches him at the Arena Tomalín, his face takes on "that brooding expression of her father's" (V259). There are marked resemblances between the two men.[41] Both have a weakness for elaborate projects that cannot be realized and for drink, and both end their careers as consuls to remote Latin American towns. The affinity between Yvonne and Geoffrey is based also on their common sense of bereavement and dispossession. Like the Consul, she thinks of herself as an orphan, "a small lone figure" bearing the curse of the Constables in her blood, and she too craves a principle of order that will render her existence intelligible: "One had never given up, or ceased to hope, or to try, gropingly, to find a meaning, a pattern, an answer—" (V268). Her marriage with the Consul has, for all its imperfections, come closer than anything else in her experience to fulfilling that need. In one of her letters, she reminds him of "what we built together," of "the structure and the beauty" (V345) that have been allowed to fall into ruin.

If only she can draw Geoffrey out of the Mexican Charybdis and induce him to attempt a new life in British Columbia, Yvonne believes, the happiness of their first days together might be reborn and grow anew. The nearest approach the couple make to a reconciliation occurs in chapter 9. A bull, his horns trapped in the railings, bellows as picadors thrust lances into his testicles. At this moment the Consul, who has identified with the beast and feels himself unmanned, leans "his damp head against her hair like a child" and agrees to accompany her "anywhere, so long as it's away...from all this." It seems that "a spirit of intercession and tenderness hover[s] over them, guarding, watching" (V277). Their rapprochement cannot endure, however, for Yvonne is *not* his mother and, try as she will, she cannot give him the unconditional love for which he yearns. The resurgence of hope, fleeting as it is, reiterates for almost the last time a major theme in the *Volcano*[42]—the one first enunciated in the epigraphs from Sophocles and Goethe—and it throws the excruciating developments of chapter 10 into bold relief.

The tenuousness of Geoffrey's promise to his wife becomes clear when he "almost absentmindedly" orders a mescal at the Salón Ofélia. This particular drink "would be the end," a familiar spirit has cautioned him, "though a damned good end perhaps" (V69–70). But the *poquito* for which he asks can hardly be classified, the Consul rationalizes, as a "serious mescal." Whether he should or should not drink is, as we have observed, an inverse variation on the question of whether he does or does not want Yvonne. The uncertainty he experiences is also comparable to "waiting for something, and then again, not waiting" (V281). His mood of evasive expectancy dissolves into a nightmarish fantasy—a foretaste of the mescal-inspired hallucinations of chapter 12—in which he recalls standing on a station platform "where after drinking all night he had gone to meet Lee Maitland ...gone, lightheaded, light-footed, and in that state of being where Baudelaire's angel indeed wakes, desiring to meet trains perhaps, but to meet no trains that stop" (V281). Geoffrey recognizes his kinship with the degenerate creatures portrayed in *L'aube spirituelle;* he too is tormented by remorse, "l'Idéal rongeur," which arouses "dans la brute assoupie un ange."[43] Lee Maitland represents "another angel,...a fair-haired one" (V281), possibly "l'ange plein de gaîté" of *Réversibilité,*[44] who can scarcely be expected to comprehend the nameless terrors of the protagonist's night.

The identity of the person he awaits is as shadowy as Godot's, but her advent, were it to occur, would appear to signal a momentous change in his affairs. It seems likely that this "fair Virginian"—is it she who has flung the soiled tissues from a passing train?—symbolizes eternal womanhood in both its ideal and fatal aspects. The mixed emotions with which Geoffrey contemplates Lee's arrival are plainly a reflection of his ambivalence toward Yvonne, who is also at once "angel and destroyer."[45] Insofar as these feminine figures correspond to the imago, they generate the combination of desire and inhibition we have explored in connection with the Consul's impotence in the third chapter. Viewed in this light, many details of his fantasy—for example, the tree that resembles an "exploding sea-mine, frozen," or the "dead lamps" in Vavin whose art nouveau contortions recall "erect snakes poised to strike" (V282)—disclose the anxiety he feels at the prospect of intercourse. Dismay over his sexual inadequacy becomes most acute when he imagines himself assembling a bouquet with which to welcome the angel: "But the embankment flowers would not pick, spurting sap, sticky, the flowers were on the wrong end of the stalks" (V282).

Beyond Geoffrey's dread of coitus, the little death, lies a still deeper apprehension, an intimation of mortality. The "terrible trains" that race past—"each wailing for its demon lover" (V283), like the damsel in Coleridge's dream vision—cry out to him from that "deep romantic chasm"[46] where ecstasy verges on oblivion. All of these trains are expresses, and according to Mexican law "a corpse will be transported by express" (V43, 284). Morbid as the Consul's imaginings may be, they contain an element of reassurance as well. The fact that the trains do not stop is in itself consoling, for it suspends the exigencies of both sexual performance and dying.[47] His memories of sitting in a station tavern trying to comfort Mr. Quattras and of his having saved the Barbados bookie from deportation—"that battle against death had been won" (V283–84)—tend to corroborate this reading. The entire fantasy serves as a justification for his having had the mescal: "he was now fully awake, fully sober again, and well able to cope with anything that might come his way" (V284) Indeed the drink appears self-vindicating, for its initial effect is to dissipate fears about its ultimate consequences.

However much anguish the angel's detraining might cause the protagonist, there is a corner of his psyche that yearns profoundly for her coming and for the transfiguration it promises. Moments do occur, as we have seen, when he tries desperately to summon the manhood needed in order to be a proper husband, to fulfill the dream of a new life that he shares with Yvonne. One may construe even his appeals for maternal tenderness as evidence less of an urge to cede his responsibilities than of a desire to renew his courage. It is fitting that his thoughts should turn from the "fair Virginian" to the matrix of all such imagos; at no time does the Consul command our respect and sympathy more fully than when he prays—or attempts to pray—to the compassionate Virgin who has answered his plea for Yvonne's return:

> "Nothing is altered and in spite of God's mercy I am still
> alone. Though my suffering seems senseless I am still in
> agony. There is no explanation of my life." Indeed there was
> not, nor was this what he'd meant to convey. . . . "Please let
> me make her happy, deliver me from this dreadful tyranny of
> self. I have sunk low. Let me sink lower still, that I may know
> the truth. Teach me to love again, to love life." That
> wouldn't do either. . . . "Give me back my purity, the knowl-
> edge of the Mysteries, that I have betrayed and lost.—Let me
> be truly lonely, that I may honestly pray. Let us be happy
> again somewhere, if it's only together, if it's only out of this
> terrible world. Destroy the world!" he cried in his heart.
> (V289)

The prayer is that of a soul Baudelairean in its division.[48] In the same moment Geoffrey pleads for bliss and suffering, commu- nion and banishment, love and annihilation. Searching for the light, he asks to be allowed a still deeper katabasis into the void. Proud and contrite, his spirit rends itself, and one half mocks the other's supplication. The Consul, a failed theurgist, has severed himself from the roots of faith: his heart is closed to charity, both human and divine. Only mescal, which he drinks as though he were "taking an eternal sacrament" (V40), allays the resulting spiritual dryness.

"To drink or not to drink" (V287), that is the question haunting Geoffrey Firmin. Does it lie within his power to resist the forces that conduce to an affirmative response? At some point between habit and addiction he might still have done so, but by 2 November 1938 his alcoholism has acquired a momentum sufficient to engulf any vectors of will, internal or external, that oppose it. Even in the course of that one day, the prospect of a drink at the Farolito comes more and more to possess his thoughts and to diminish the options available. That his good angel has retreated to the wings is evident when he erupts in open mockery of his wife's salvage operations: " 'Geoffrey darling, why don't you stop drinking, it isn't too late.... Why isn't it? Did I say so?' What was he saying? The Consul listened to himself almost in surprise at this sudden cruelty, this vulgarity.... Must he say it? —It seemed he must. 'For all you know it's only the knowledge that it most certainly is too late that keeps me alive at all' " (V312). His need to deflect Yvonne's tender concern stems from the early loss of his parents' love, which leads him both to fear any relationship involving a comparable hazard and, as we have seen, to reenact the disaster in compulsive fashion. Precisely because their marriage had been "too good, too horribly unimaginable to lose," it has become "impossible finally to bear" (V201). Geoffrey realizes, at the same time, that *no se puede vivir sin amar*. He can avoid the risk of privation only by consigning himself to certain perdition.[49] At the end of chapter 10, the Consul gives voice to the resolve that has long been shaping itself in his heart: "I love hell. I can't wait to get back there. In fact I'm running" (V314). Implicit in his choice is the doleful assumption that one can spite death by refusing to live.

Geoffrey's assent to damnation may be less thoroughgoing than it first appears—"the queer thing was, he wasn't quite serious" (V314)—but it marks, nonetheless, a crucial turn in the novel. The denouement presented in the last two chapters follows as inexorably as any in modern fiction. In them Lowry seeks for his characters a niche in eternity. Yvonne gazes at the "jewelled wheels of countless unmeasured galaxies, turning, turning, majestically, into infinity" (V322), and attempts to decipher the meaning of her own life and that of the Consul. In her cosmology the Pleiades do not flee from the bibulous Orion, as they do in Apollodorus's account, but rather fly toward him, no doubt in order to help combat the Scorpion, whose sting brings death to itself and others.[50]

Toward the close of chapter 11 lightning strikes in the dark wood that adjoins Parián. "There is always a door left open in the mind—as men have been known in great thunderstorms to leave their real doors open for Jesus to walk in—for the entrance and the reception of the unprecedented, the fearful acceptance of the thunderbolt that never falls on oneself," reflects the narrator, "and it was through this mental door that Yvonne...now perceived that something was menacingly wrong" (V334). The lightning coincides with the murder of Geoffrey, and it causes the horse he has untethered to bolt for the forest. It is this horse, stolen from the dying Indian, that threatens Yvonne. As the riderless beast rears above her, she beholds a series of figures in the saddle, among them her estranged husband, whose lost potency appears to have returned in the form of malign energy. "Could Thomas Hardy do as much?"[51] the author demands. And indeed one discovers a comparable tendency to apocalyptic extremes in the two novelists, especially in the way they handle their finales.

But the symbolic correspondences cataloged above by no means exhaust Lowry's store. "The very end of the chapter has," he acknowledges, "practically stepped outside the bounds of the book altogether"[52] Yvonne imagines herself "suddenly gathered upwards and borne towards the stars, through eddies of stars scattering aloft with ever wider circlings like rings on water"

(V336). Recalling her film career in Hollywood, one might suppose that the ecstatic prose in which this ascent to the Pleiades is cast subjects the starlet in her to irony. Perhaps it does, but if so the irony is of the gentle sort that frames Félicité's apotheosis in *Un coeur simple.* Both Lowry and Flaubert bestow salvation in a manner consonant with their heroines' vision of the world.

Chapters 11 and 12, the action of which occurs in the hour following sundown, point backward several hundred pages and forward one year to the first chapter. One may conceive of all three as movements in the symphonic form of what Joyce called "cyclewheeling history," a seamless composition whose themes and counterthemes appear time and again in a karmic circumfluence. Of the many motifs that bind these chapters together the most important center on Yvonne and Geoffrey's abortive communications. We learn from the Consul's unposted letter, written in the Farolito, that he has received a number of missives from his wife but that his mind has not been lucid enough to apprehend anything more than their grossest features. In chapter 11 Yvonne discovers, on the back of a menu, an unfinished sonnet "of a wavering and collapsed design" (V330). The poem, which is in Geoffrey's hand and speaks of "strange hellish tales," recalls the lines from *Doctor Faustus* on which Jacques broods just before he finds his friend's letter (composed, it would seem, during the same spree). In analogous fashion, Yvonne's perusal of the lyric anticipates her husband's recovery in chapter 12 of the missing letters she has sent him, the very ones that have prompted the reply Laruelle reads in chapter 1. *Under the Volcano* thus resembles a serpent biting its own tail. Lowry's comparison of his book to a cathedral in the churrigueresque or overloaded manner, with its first and last chapters as the towers, is at most a slight hyperbole.[53]

The parallel sentiments expressed in the Firmins' correspondence indicate the possibilities, now forfeit, they have had for a rapprochement. Especially poignant are their appeals to the mystical sense of unity—the "self we created, apart from us" (V40)—

that prevailed during the early days of their marriage. As Geoffrey sits in the Farolito, attentive at last to what his wife has written, a wave of tenderness and remorse overcomes him. There in the cantina, miserably desiring and not desiring Yvonne, he encounters the whore María.[54] Her name suggests that other Mary to whom he has addressed the petition in chapter 10, and in the dim light her aspect resembles Yvonne's.

The Consul regards María as a Lilith figure, "a fiendish apparatus for calamitous sickening sensation" (V349). With so profane an avatar of the feminine, he becomes once again capable of intercourse. Parián has seemed to promise a "healing love" but leads instead to a final "unprophylactic rejection" of grace, an act for which the protagonist must accept full responsibility: "He could prevent it even now. He would not prevent it" (V348). Geoffrey's copulation with María seals his doom as surely as the demonic union with Helena has Faustus's. If only for "brutal hygienic reasons," the Consul observes, he is obliged to forswear any hope of rejoining Yvonne. Overtones of spiritual defilement attach to syphilis in Lowry's novel much as they do in Mann's *Doktor Faustus*. Like Adrian Leverkühn, Geoffrey draws from this "ultimate contamination" a kind of strength, the freedom "to devour what remained of his life in peace" (V354).[55]

Perhaps as a consequence of his Wesleyan schooling, the Consul is at heart a puritan. He refers to Yvonne's illicit lovers as "ninneyhammers with gills like codfish and veins like racehorses" (V313), and, in the midst of his betrayal of her, he thinks no better of his own "crucified evil organ." The act of passion is for him an agony, a moment of suffering so intense that out of it, he feels, "something must be born, and what would be born was his own death" (V349). Unfortunately the sacrifice of Geoffrey Firmin, the guilt-laden *cabrón*, is without expiatory power. Rather it increases the burden of sin, for if the deed turns his final hour into a perverse *imitatio Christi*[56] and if María represents the Virgin degraded to the level of succubus, then his coupling with her may be construed as a singularly blasphemous form of incest.

Becoming one's own father is a crucial aim of the oedipal project, but it is an aspiration fiercely opposed by the superego, the agent of one's actual sire. The harsh justice of the psyche thus demands that Geoffrey deliver himself into the hands of the authorities for punishment. And indeed the Unión Militar chiefs await him with their verdict. He is, in their eyes, an "antichrista" from whom no cup shall be taken until the bitterest dregs have been drained.

It may be that María is "an abstraction merely," a cipher whose significance the Consul creates in his own mind, but that is not to say that he can alter the terms of his vision and avert disaster. Sundered from the divine "pharos of the world," he has no means of finding his way back from "a place where even love could not penetrate, and save in the thickest flames there was no courage" (V201). In the Farolito, a lighthouse that misguides the voyager, Geoffrey meditates for the last time on the saving innocence of the northern forests, "an undiscovered, perhaps an undiscoverable Paradise, that might have been a solution, to return there, to build . . . a new life with Yvonne. Why hadn't he thought of it before?" (V353). And then he half-remembers that he has, while sitting in this very cantina. The destructive drive has eradicated all but the faintest traces of his letter. With Eridanus denied the Consul, the Parián wilderness becomes for him an ersatz Eden, "the paradise of his despair" (V338). His last playful and pathetic gesture in the direction of a new life consists in telling the Chief of Gardens that his name is William Blackstone, and indeed at several points in the novel he identifies himself with this pioneer Adam, who found the constraints of the Bay colony so intolerable that he preferred instead to live among the Indians.

Throughout his long last day the Consul aims verbal thrusts at those who would interfere with the bearing his daemon has set for him. In the end, just before he is murdered, he spends his rage in an outright physical assault on his enemies. Various leaders among the semifascist *brutos* represent both the violence and corruption of public life and the loathsome side of his own character. He finds in the Chief of Rostrums' visage "a hint of M. Laruelle," his treacherous alter ego, and lashes out at it, as he does at his principal tormentor, the Jefe de Jardineros, who figures forth "the image of himself . . . at the crossroads of his career" (V359). The scene has by this time turned utterly Kafkaesque.[57] These figures in the Farolito are not so much human beings as they are the masks of dark forces thrusting up from the psychic depths. Geoffrey's attack culminates in a maudlin, deranged, beatific *j'accuse* in which he is no longer fully aware of what he is saying: "Only the poor, only through God, only the people you wipe your feet on, the poor in spirit, old men carrying their fathers and philosophers weeping in the dust, . . . if you'd only stop interfering, stop walking in your sleep, stop sleeping with my wife, only the beggars and the accursed" (V372). The Consul's outburst is, to say the least, quixotic, but if there is anything at all redemptive in his agony it is this declaration of solidarity with the world's afflicted. His frantic efforts to release the Indian's horse indicate a profound yearning to aid the victims of repression, political and psychological.

From a naturalistic standpoint Geoffrey's liberation of the horse ends in catastrophe; on the visionary plane of the novel, however, his act has more ambiguous consequences. Just as the dying Yvonne feels herself drawn upward into the celestial swirl, so the Consul undertakes in his imagination a purgatorial feat, the conquest of Popocatepetl. He carries with him on this fantastic expedition a curious assortment of gear, including brochures from the Hotel Fausto; these encumbrances, representing the past, weigh upon him and lead eventually to his collapse. Luckily a mountain rescue team is at hand, and he finds himself "in an ambulance shrieking through the jungle . . . racing uphill past the timberline toward the peak—and this was certainly one way to get there!" (V375). The pathos of his actual situation and the atonement of which he still dreams merge in surrealistic humor.

Lowry's apocalyptic final paragraphs evoke *le gouffre* as powerfully as any lines in Baudelaire. The summit Geoffrey imagines himself attaining, however unconventionally, disintegrates, and topples him into the volcanic crater. His extremity foreshadows a holocaust of immense scope, a virtual Armaggedon.[58] It strikes the Consul that the cavity is filled with erupting lava: "yet no, it wasn't the volcano, the world itself was bursting, bursting into black spouts of villages catapulted into space, with himself falling through it all, through the inconceivable pandemonium of a million tanks, through the blazing of ten million burning bodies" (V375). The plunge of Geoffrey Firmin, still clinging to his vision of a paradisiacal ascent, into the Malebolge elicits a surge of compassion and dread comparable to the one we experience when the *Pequod* sinks, with the "bird of heaven" furled in Ahab's flag, into her abyss.

As Yvonne lies beneath the rearing horse, she has the sensation of being in a ravine from which "she must escape, through the friendly forest to their house, their little home by the sea" (V336). At the same moment the Consul, hurtling into the barranca, feels as though he is falling into a wood whose trees close over him, pityingly. Thus these two star-crossed lovers join in symbols of the new life each envisions, but which is not of this world. They attain it only in a manner akin to that of the legendary Popocatepetl and Ixtaccihuatl, whose disappointed love is eternalized in the peaks overlooking Quauhnahuac, by becoming incarnate in the *Volcano*.

3
Forests of Symbols

The Later
Works

The language in which I might be able not only to write but to think is
neither Latin nor English, neither Italian nor Spanish, but a language
none of whose words is known to me, a language in which inanimate
things speak to me and wherein I may one day have to justify myself
before an unknown judge.
　　　—Hugo von Hofmannsthal, "The Letter of Lord Chandos"

Whenever I look at a mountain I always expect it to turn into a volcano.
　　　　　—Italo Svevo, "A Contract"

"We'd be awfully grateful," wrote Lowry to his agent in 1940, "if
you'd send us some news of our posthumous works."[1] An irony
much grimmer than the artist intended has overtaken that jest,
for of the six volumes of his fiction to reach print, four have
appeared since his death in 1957. Among novelists the case of
Franz Kafka comes to mind. Unfortunately the parallel between
the two writers' posthumously published books turns on their
number and the agonizing circumstances of their composition
rather than on their merits, for none of Lowry's later writings, in
the form he left them, begins to rival *Under the Volcano*. That
novel was, from the critic's standpoint, its author's passport to
immortality, but for Lowry himself it seemed at times a prema-
ture death warrant. Like Geoffrey Firmin, the artist used his
powers of imagination to destroy himself. When his persona Sigbjørn Wilderness speaks, in "Through the Panama," of a man
"not enmeshed by, but *killed* by his own book and the malign

forces it arouses,"[2] we get an inkling of the cost Lowry's art exacted. His involvement with the characters and themes of the *Volcano* was so profound that many of the things he wrote in the four or five years following its publication are more in the nature of meditations on his magnum opus than works of fiction in their own right. Along with this fixation on the *Volcano,* illness, drink, poverty, tribulations with publishers, a Kafkaesque scrupulosity, and his habit of working simultaneously on several projects combined to hinder him from bringing the bulk of his work in progress to completion.[3]

During the ten years that remained to Lowry after the appearance of the *Volcano,* he launched many narratives, all parts of the immensely ambitious sequence entitled *The Voyage that Never Ends,* and came close to finishing only one, *Hear Us O Lord from Heaven Thy Dwelling Place.* Since the *Voyage* had as its thematic skewer a recounting of the arduous task entailed by its very creation, the novelist found himself in the Shandean predicament of trying to tell a story that was forever outstripping his capacity to render it. Among the works discussed in the first chapter, *Lunar Caustic* continued to figure in his plans and so, as a rule, did *Ultramarine,* although he remained somewhat skeptical about the prospects for salvaging the latter. Two novels inspired by a return visit to Mexico in 1945–46, *Dark as the Grave Wherein My Friend Is Laid* and *La Mordida,* draw nearly all their force from renewed confrontations with the Consul's demons. Douglas Day and Margerie Lowry have collated the extant drafts of *Dark as the Grave* and hewn them into a tolerably coherent narrative. The manuscript of *La Mordida,* consisting mainly of roughly drawn scenes of tourist troubles in Acapulco and Mexico City, together with ruminations on everything under the tropical sun, is too disconnected to warrant publication.

In spite of having the *Volcano* as a "diabolic battery" at its center, the *Voyage* was to conclude, paradoxically, by rising above tragedy. The "resolution should be triumphant," notes Wilderness in "Through the Panama": "That is to say it is certainly in my power to make it so" (H39). This echo of the Consul's challenge to Jacques—Jacques?—indicates the measure of self-doubt to which the artist was prey. The victorious reversal was to have occurred in *La Mordida*,[4] yet the draft of that novel, which ends with the protagonist and his wife being expelled from Mexico, contains little to sustain the aspiration. "The Forest Path to the Spring," written "in terms of enthusiasm and high seriousness usually reserved for catastrophe and tragedy" (H271), attains the transcendence Lowry was seeking more fully than any of his other narratives. The novella constitutes a handsome scenario for *Eridanus*, a book-length treatment of the Columbian Eden myth that never got far beyond the planning stage. Much of the material the artist had gathered for that project, along with the theme of responsibility for another's suicide first explored in a fragmentary work called *The Ordeal of Sigbjørn Wilderness*, found its way into *October Ferry to Gabriola*, the novel that he hoped would provide a fitting encore to the *Volcano*. His widow has reduced the nearly three thousand surviving pages of notes and drafts to the version of *October Ferry* published in 1970. Whatever faults the *oeuvres posthumes* may have, they do illumine the cast of Lowry's mind, the circumstances in which he wrote, and the new terrain he was staking out for his art in the final years of his life. Furthermore, several of the shorter narratives—"Ghostkeeper" in *Psalms and Songs,* a mélange of pieces by and about Lowry, and "The Bravest Boat," "Strange Comfort Afforded by the Profession" and "The Forest Path to the Spring" in *Hear Us O Lord*—have substantial intrinsic worth. Indeed "The Forest Path" ranks as an impressive contribution to a genre in which distinction has been rare, the mode of pastoral confession whose prototype is *Walden.*

For Lowry relinquishing control over any of his projects engendered an unusually keen sort of anxiety. It is not surprising, then, that his submission of the fourth and final version of the *Volcano* to publishers in June 1945 left him feeling vacant and dejected. His composition of the novel had been an effort to transcend the horrors he had undergone in Mexico and, at the same time, to render those memories more vivid, for they afforded him the kind of intense masochistic relish so evident in the character of Geoffrey Firmin. With the completion of his book, the phantoms of the author's late twenties threatened to abandon him to disconsolate middle age. The means he chose for prolonging the experience that had been his artistic and emotional capital for almost a decade was a return to its source. Lowry and his second wife, Margerie, departed from British Columbia in November and spent the next five months sojourning in Mexico City, Cuernavaca, Acapulco, and Oaxaca. By mid-1947 the novelist had begun to convert the travel diaries they had kept into *Dark as the Grave*. "I'm writing what can fairly be described as a good book," he reported to his editor. "We progress towards equilibrium this time instead of in the opposite direction, and the result is considerably more exciting, if not even more horrible."[5] He worked intermittently on *Dark as the Grave* until 1952, at which point the "bolus"—a 705-page typescript consisting of three narrative drafts, memoranda relating to further revisions, and a sequence of poems that the artist meant to attribute to his protagonist— was deposited in the vault of a Vancouver bank where it remained when, two years later, he left Canada for the last time. Thus Lowry effectively, if not wittingly, forsook his novel.

The drafts from which Douglas Day and Margerie Lowry drew their edition of *Dark as the Grave* are, for the most part, variations on one another. They contain little evidence of the kind one discovers in the successive versions of *Under the Volcano* that the work was truly in progress. The editors deleted repetitions, loose ends, and aimless dialogue, then arranged the remnants into what is virtually a collage. They included no apparatus, aside from Day's general introduction, to indicate just where and in accordance with what logic these excisions and transpositions were made.[6] Lowry himself composed in a similar mosaic fashion, and Margerie, who was involved in almost every phase of her husband's literary endeavors, knew his intentions as no other human being could. He regularly asked her, when the writing was going badly, to draft a "Margie version" and frequently adopted her suggestions. But the question remains whether anybody, even a person as intimately concerned as Margerie Lowry, is entitled to make substantive changes in a dead writer's work, and at least among academic critics the consensus is that no one has that right.[7] Since few readers have ready access to the manuscripts in the University of British Columbia Library, however, we are obliged *faute de mieux* to direct our attention to the published text.

In *Dark as the Grave* one finds little of the opulent style and none of the labyrinthine structure that characterize the *Volcano*. Occasionally there is a Melvillean period reminiscent of that earlier glory, such as the following aerial view of the Mexican ranges:

> Up, up, they climbed, ever higher into the Sierra Madre, mountains beyond mountains beyond mountains, where on those mountains the farmers sowed their seed crops and left them, upon seemingly inaccessible peaks—far below, there were even signs of cultivation—and where, the stewardess told them, the farmers sowed once and just left their crops to fructify, without even bothering to keep an eye on them, not looking at them for a year at a time, when they would pay a difficult pilgrimage up there, making the occasion doubtless one of celebration, at which period they would be found to have flourished splendidly, as did Parsifal's flowers in his absence. (D68)

These summits are encompassed, however, by vast stretches of prose so flat and arid one hesitates to quote from it. At other moments the writing descends into excruciating self-parody, for instance, when the protagonist likens a hotel elevator to "a station of the cross, in the unfinished Oberammergau of his life" (D77-78). *Longueurs* and lapses of taste abound in the early drafts of the *Volcano* too, but comparatively few remain in the final version. Although it is conceivable that had Lowry resumed work on *Dark as the Grave* he might eventually have accomplished a similar transformation of it, there is little in either the manuscripts or the published text to encourage that supposition.

No current strong enough to draw things to an ineluctable end runs through *Dark as the Grave*. The narrative consists rather of incidents, many of which strike the reader as essentially random in character, related in linear chronological fashion. Of a piece with this slackness of plot is a protagonist whose own world design has begun to unravel. The author's persona, Sigbjørn Wilderness,[8] feels that he must "make some excuse or explanation for being on earth at all" (D11) and that "if he did not hold on to himself he would disappear altogether" (D16). As we have seen, the Consul is also desperately insecure with regard to his being-in-the-world; his story unfolds, however, in an atmosphere of doom that makes even the smallest details seem parts of an inexorable process. Ostensibly Sigbjørn journeys to Mexico in order to still dissonant echoes of his past, but what he wishes at bottom to do is revive the "old consciousness of fatality" (D210) that had lent form and purpose to his existence.

Wilderness has recently completed *The Valley of the Shadow of Death,* a novel in every respect parallel to the *Volcano,* and he fears that now, with the book done, the landscape that has been central to his vision may cease to resonate symbolically. Even Popocatepetl and Ixtaccihuatl threaten to become merely themselves, "just volcanoes, dead and extinct" (D164), with no legendary significance. This attrition he seeks to resist by treating *The Valley of the Shadow,* an edifice built upon youthful experience, as the blueprint for his maturity. Thus Sigbjørn, aboard a bus that winds down the mountainside into Cuernavaca, imagines himself reading "a book that . . . had not yet been wholly written, and probably never would be, but that was, in some transcendental manner, *being* written as they went along" (D103). That his life and art take their contours from a numinous force field he infers from the proleptic nature of passages in his novel, signs that he has "become his own 'character'" (D119).[9] There are indeed some remarkable coincidences, such as his wife Primrose's renting an apartment in the Quinta Dolores, apparently without knowing that it had been the model for Laruelle's tower, or the *borracho*'s assault on a blind woman who clutches a dead dog "exhumed out of *The Valley of the Shadow*" (D101), but it never seems to occur to Wilderness that these correspondences might be explained without recourse to the supernatural. To do so would, in his eyes, constitute a breach of poetic faith.

Sigbjørn's vocation as a writer gives his existence whatever meaning it has, yet he finds himself "haunted by the suspicion . . . that he was destined to copy all his life" (D24). His anxiety stems, in this instance, from a sense that the appearance of Charles Jackson's *The Lost Weekend,* referred to in the novel as *Drunkard's Rigadoon,* has invalidated the claims he wishes to make for himself as an explorer of the alcoholic Inferno. That apprehension is as groundless as his creator's fear that *Ultramarine* was merely a pastiche of Aiken and Grieg. For Wilderness, as for Lowry himself, the true peril lies not in emulating others' work but rather his own: *Dark as the Grave* remains unintelligible apart from the book it mirrors. Flaubert and Joyce admonished the artist to be, like God in the creation, invisible. Lowry, on the other hand, seems to have preferred the more narcissistic satisfaction of abiding, "almost Godlike," in the midst of his handiwork.

Dark as the Grave may be radically flawed by its dependence on the *Volcano,* but it does provide us with intriguing data on the genesis of that novel. We learn, for example, that chapter 12, set in the Farolito, was written immediately after the composition of the Tomalín road episode, the germ of the book, and that both are based quite closely on actual occurrences. (Lowry was not averse to cultivating his own legend, but few of his glosses on the *Volcano* have the ring of fabrication.) The macaronic dialogue in the last chapter derives from an encounter in a Cuernavaca bar: "I had been myself up to the Universal and fallen in conversation with a bunch of complete borrachos, who far from being annoyed that I copied down every word they said in a notebook seemed flattered by this. They were attempting to talk English. I myself, Spanish: and the resultant confusion was precisely what I wanted" (D151). The equally remarkable dialogue between the Consul and the Chief of Rostrums—"You are no a de wrider, you are de espider, and we shoota de espiders in Méjico"[10]—originated in an interview that took place during a Christmas week sojourn in the Oaxaca jail. One might reasonably suppose that Geoffrey's copulation with the whore María was the author's invention, merely a step in the perverse logic of his hero's self-damnation, yet it too appears to have a biographical foundation. The novelist recalls that, while the final separation from his first wife was being arranged, "he slept with prostitute after prostitute with passion such as he had never known until then in an effort to...connect his suffering with something" (D87).[11] At heart he is as much a puritan as his Consul, tormented by "supermodesty" and worried about "his tool hanging out" (D193). The contrast between this frank vulgarity and the lyric heightening of such matters in the *Volcano* indicates the kind of alembication Lowry's primary experience has undergone in his finished work.

Character drawing was not, the novelist told Jonathan Cape,[12] one of his major concerns; nonetheless, he did manage to invest the principal figures in the *Volcano* with enough of his personality to make them live. Yvonne remains largely an *anima* projection, but even she is sufficiently realized to perform her role successfully. One cannot say the same for *Dark as the Grave,* in which the author identifies himself so thoroughly with Sigbjørn Wilderness that he has almost no vitality to spare for his other characters. In her husband's eyes, Primrose is "a girl like a flame" (D161). Although she is supposedly a woman of thirty-nine, her response to Mexico is in fact that of a breathless ingénue. Whatever substance she has derives from her relation to Sigbjørn, who relies on her to attend to all his practical needs, including the procurement of his whiskey. As one might suspect, this dependence causes considerable friction. "If only she would be sensible," Sigbjørn reflects, "and treat [my] drinking as Dostoevski's second wife did his gambling" (D133). He is ambivalent in the manner of a small boy who demands maternal support and, at the same time, resents the person who gives it. In this respect, Wilderness comes close to being a textbook alcoholic.[13] Lowry sought to avoid making his heroine into an Astarte like Faulkner's Eula or Joyce's Molly,[14] although nowhere in his canon is there any indication that he could have done so had he wanted to. Primrose was to represent "the spiritual life principle, still allied to the earth, once one of the elements" (D202). Unfortunately her bond with the earth is all too slender, and she remains a nearly bloodless abstraction. The Primrose who appears in *La Mordida* is a somewhat rounder character, especially in the scenes of marital discord which punctuate that unpublished novel.[15]

Juan Fernando Martínez, the only other figure worth noting in *Dark as the Grave,* exists almost wholly as a function of the protagonist's consciousness. Fernando is indeed a ghost of the past, having been in the grave for six years, although Sigbjørn, who has come to Mexico anticipating a reunion with him, does not learn of his friend's death until the next to last chapter. The Zapotecan had served as the model for two characters in Wilderness's novel. As a fieldworker for the Banco Ejidal, Fernando had lent some of his attributes—his "wild courage, humility, and greatness of soul" (D221)—to Hugh's idol, the peasant leader Juan Cerillo. And in another of his roles, that of cantina philosopher, he had left his imprint on Geoffrey's comrade in drink Dr. Vigil. (The brothers Firmin were intended, said Lowry, "to be aspects of the same man,"[16] and it seems that this axiom extends to their friends as well.) Both sides of Fernando's nature appeal to Sigbjørn; however, the one associated with the Farolito and "the old wine of complete despair" (D210) represents, through most of the book, the more potent attraction. Could it be, the protagonist asks himself, that their relationship was "but another manifestation of his secret desire for death?" (D223) It is not altogether strange, then, that upon hearing of his alter ego's demise Wilderness experiences feelings of both grief and release. Fernando, murdered in a Villahermosa bar, has met the Consul's end and thus, for the time being at least, spared Sigbjørn the necessity of acting it out himself. Moreover, the Zapotecan's self-immolation is efficacious in a way that Geoffrey's could never be, for he has offered it not only in death but in life as well. Through his work for agrarian reform he has merged his identity with the larger rhythm of life, *la vida impersonal.* Signs of the new birth to which Fernando's efforts have given rise are all about the Wildernesses as they depart from Oaxaca: "Everywhere one saw rich green fields, felt a sense of fruitfulness, and of the soil responding and of men living as they ought to live,...but they never could have done it without the Banco's help.... The Banco Ejidal had become a garden" (D254–55). That the concluding pages of the novel may strike the reader as an idealized assessment of the green revolution matters less than Lowry's failure to do more than outline the character of Fernando's sacrifice. Far from being dramatically or poetically established, its value is merely asserted. Clearly we are dealing at this point with an exceedingly rough version.

Under the Volcano is no less autobiographical in origin than *Dark as the Grave,* yet one feels that at every crucial turn the former follows the *cammin di nostra vita,* the route of broadest significance, whereas the latter remains, as Lowry acknowledged, "a sidestreet to [his] own consciousness."[17] How the *Volcano* came to be written and the experiences its composition entailed are surely worth relating; whether the novel constitutes the proper vehicle for that account is another matter. *Dark as the Grave* might have been a better, more honest book had the author explicitly abandoned fiction and worked in a mode similar to that of Gide's *Journal des faux-monnayeurs* or Mann's *Entstehung des Doktor Faustus.* Lowry does cast "Through the Panama" as a journal, and, although he is not entirely master of the form in that story, it appears a much more effective means of rendering a journey that coincides with a crisis of artistic self-encapsulation than the one he employs in *Dark as the Grave.*

Many forms coalesce in the *Volcano* to give the book its richness. "It can be regarded as a kind of symphony," remarked the author, "or in another way as a kind of opera—or even a horse opera. It is hot music, a poem, a song, a tragedy, a comedy, a farce, . . . a prophecy, a political warning, a cryptogram, a preposterous movie, and a writing on the wall."[18] But whatever else the *Volcano* may be, it is, finally, a novel capable of a sustained and intensive probing of mental and moral life. As Lowry gradually disengaged from that book, he also found himself withdrawing more and more from the novel form. His perception of the world appears to have narrowed considerably during those years as a result of his deepening estrangement from a society whose "ugliness and complete baffling sterility" (H44) were enough, he felt, to drive a sensitive man to drink or at least to furnish him with an excuse for indulging what was, on purely personal grounds, a formidable urge. The artist had, as a young man, been able to yield to alcoholic temptations while preserving his capacity to write and even heightening his wit and imagination. In his forties Lowry no longer possessed the same resiliency: he could still conceive extended narratives in broad outline, but his power to execute such designs had been impaired.[19] The life in Canada that is the theme of *October Ferry to Gabriola* seems to be matter nearly as promising for fiction as his youthful adventures in Mexico had been, but he never recovered, except for brief intervals, the aesthetic distance and discipline that had allowed him to consummate *Under the Volcano.*

Lowry often tried to deceive himself regarding his work, but by mid-1953 he was obliged to admit that *October Ferry* had "not one single conventional virtue" of the novel form: "its character drawing is virtually non-existent, symbols are pointed at blatantly instead of being concealed or subsumed in the material, . . . and some readers—if they read it once—might have to read it five times before they could be convinced anything has happened at all."[20] These apparent flaws were deliberate, he claimed, for *October Ferry* was "not intended to fall into any particular category or obey any of the normal rules of a novel."[21] Many works of fiction do not observe novelistic conventions, and yet underlying them one can almost always discern alternate paradigms. In *October Ferry* there are numerous traces of the confession and the romance as Northrop Frye defines them;[22] nevertheless, the artist was unable to employ either these or any other forms with sufficient rigor to guide himself in constructing the book, or the reader in assimilating its meaning. Lowry feared and perhaps half-hoped that his narrative would come alive "for the wrong reason, . . . namely, the bloody agony of the writer writing it is so patently extreme that it creates a kind of power in itself."[23] His intuition has proved to be correct. *October Ferry* represents an attempt to work through neurotic problems the author could resolve neither in art nor apart from it. The margins of his manuscripts are filled with petitions to Saint Jude, the patron of desperate causes. Lowry recognized that Hermann Broch's remarks on Goethe applied to him: "One can imagine that Goethe, after Werther's death, had once for all conquered any suicidal tendencies of his own. No less conceivable is the fact that wherever a poet fails to incorporate his emotions completely into his literary work, and thus to neutralize them in actual life, the fate of his protagonists will become his own."[24] The difficulties in which Lowry was enmeshed—uppermost among them an impulse to self-annihilation—do, as he foresaw, rend the fictional veil and make themselves baldly and poignantly felt. Perhaps the most fruitful way to respond to this book, whose biographical overtones are more compelling than its vision or artistry, is to refine and coordinate the insights it offers into the malaise that Lowry shared with his persona.

Unlike most of the protagonists in the later fiction, Ethan Llewelyn is not portrayed as an expatriate English writer but rather as a native-born Canadian attorney, although when we encounter him on 7 October 1949, the time present of the narrative, he has not been practicing law for more than two years. The discovery that a client of whose innocence he had been convinced was in fact guilty of murder has shaken his faith in his professional acuity, reopened old wounds in his psyche, and led him to undertake a therapeutic retreat in the woods of British Columbia. There are few signs that Ethan's vocation is authentic. He does occasionally reflect on cases he has handled or on larger questions of justice, but never in much depth. The point at which his mind appears most thoroughly steeped in the law occurs in the "Useful Knots" chapter:

> Ethan's method of thinking. . .involved a process akin to composition: not as though he had been composing a brief, exactly, but had been loosely composing a mental dossier, preparatory to making a brief on behalf of an accused he proposed to defend. But the actual and frightening and certain knowledge at this moment that he had been *consciously* deceiving himself all morning, actually suppressing and misrepresenting the very events of his life for the sake of making them fit into a bearable pattern, came with the force of a revelation. If the first consciousness was the counsel for the defense, this second was the counsel for the prosecution.[25]

The style of this meditation may be as convoluted as a lawyer's, but the legal terms are plainly metaphors for psychological processes. It is not the law of Canada that concerns him so much as it is the primitive code of his own superego, which admits no appeals. By attributing a calling remote from his own to Ethan, the artist apparently meant to endow him with a measure of autonomy. In actuality the protagonist of *October Ferry* is as little distinguished from his creator as Sigbjørn Wilderness has been. Each is in essence a poet-mystic, a Kierkegaardian figure whose soul has become "sick almost to death" (F210).

That Lowry's world design was so constricted as to preclude imaginative penetration into the lives of others makes itself evident in the shallowness of his secondary characters. Ethan's wife

Jacqueline is described as "slim and supple, dark-eyed, dark-haired, and incredibly young and passionate-looking." Neither the author nor his persona are "capable of more detailed asseverations in regard to women" (F12). At times rather facile allusions serve in lieu of action or exposition to establish Jacqueline's role: she is Francesca to Ethan's Paolo, Catherine to his Heathcliff, Miranda to his Ferdinand. The last of these analogies is extended to include her father, the Prospero of *October Ferry*. Angus McCandless, the chieftain of his clan and a white magician, thinks of "nothing else but the great 'Plan' of the universe... [and] of himself, if with a saving Highland cynicism, as a single factor whose conduct vitally affected it" (F31).[26] The McCandless's cabalistic pursuits and comic high spirits correspond closely enough to the artist's own that he might have brought the Scotsman fully to life had not death truncated his work on the book. The Llewelyns differ from other couples in Lowry's fiction in that they have a child, Tommy; the boy spends most of his time away at boarding school, however, and even when he is home his parents are too preoccupied with their own difficulties to take much note of him. Many chapters go by without Tommy's being mentioned at all. Ethan has himself been a neglected child, and he passes the legacy of deprivation along, quite unconsciously, to his son.

Comparatively little is revealed to us about Ethan's boyhood, but enough that we can pinpoint several of the roots of his neurosis. His mother and father appear to have been extraordinarily cold-hearted. "Nearly the only kind action he could recall on the part of either of his parents" (F8) was the gift of a toy model of Moscow, and even that had been taken from him after a single evening. Ethan associates this retraction with his mother's death; the loss of the "magic bulbar city" corresponds to the withholding and, ultimately, the total withdrawal of her love. Like Lowry himself, the protagonist has suffered from ulcerated corneas that caused him to be nearly blind from his ninth through thirteenth years. His father has attributed this condition to "certain dirty schoolboy habits" and attempted to cure it with a razor strop, at the same time telling the boy that his supposed vice, "which had probably already led to complete impoverishment of his blood, would result in atrophy, complete idiocy and finally death at the age of nineteen" (F23). Few sons have had more reason for experiencing castration anxiety.[27] Such harsh treatment has also given rise to Ethan's unrelenting superego, necessary to constrain the murderous resentment he feels toward his father. One need scarcely wonder that, having turned this rage inward, he is profoundly uneasy about occupying the family mansion when it eventually becomes his. The sense of being an unworthy heir leads him to construe the fire that destroys the house in May 1946 as a sign of his damnation, the flaming sword of the angel that marks his irrevocable exclusion from the parental bourne. That fire may represent a purifying ordeal occurs to him as well, but this second possibility has far less imaginative force than the first. Ethan remains childlike in his propensity to magical thinking: wishes are assumed to have a potency so great that, without mediation, they affect the objects toward which they are directed.[28] This notion may be absurd as a way of accounting for the combustion of a house, but when the desire is for punishment, its object the self, and the ego defenses are as infirm as Llewelyn's, there is indeed little to impede the transaction.

The most likely responses to the sort of parental rejection to which Ethan has been subjected are resignation and guilt. Of the two, the latter is probably the less disastrous, for the assumption of responsibility—even in reverse fashion, with the victim rather than the malefactor bearing the burden—preserves some hope that what has been done might be undone. It is this second course that Ethan follows most of the time. His guilt stems from the ambivalence, the combination of animosity with a residual yearning for atonement, that manifests itself in dreams where "his father's loneliness...he had done so little to assuage and his own childhood loneliness...merged" (F72). In order to prevent remorse from inundating his entire world, the unconscious has deflected a large portion of it into a narrow channel, the obsession centering on Peter Cordwainer's death.[29] Ethan has encouraged his college friend to take his own life, or at least it seems he has. 7 October 1949 is not only the nineteenth or twentieth anniversary of Peter's suicide—there is a discrepancy in the text as to the year (F58, 211)—but it is also the centenary of Poe's death, and Ethan's recollections of the Cordwainer affair, embroidered with many "senseless inventions" (F50), do in fact carry the imprint of a macabre imagination reminiscent of Poe's. Since Peter has been one of those who harassed Ethan at school while his vision was weak, it is quite possible that the latter has harbored a longing for vengeance. In view of his disposition to equate the wish with the deed, this desire might be sufficient to actuate feelings of guilt without his having had any real complicity in his classmate's suicide. Certainly the two experiences are linked in Ethan's mind: "his whole life since the business of Peter Cordwainer had been in the nature of a self-inflicted penance, just as what had happened to him in childhood had been a similar penance, only inflicted on him from outside" (F41). That the later punishment is "self-inflicted" suggests a thorough identification on Ethan's part with the victim: had he not "secretly admired Cordwainer for what he had done" (F50) and does he not remember—whether accurately or not is irrelevant—having made the following promise: "I'll come later. The same way" (F69)? Peter's death, like that of Fernando, represents an offering to the protagonist's furies. But in *October Ferry,* if not in *Dark as the Grave,* the hero's sense of having incurred a debt that must some day be discharged continues to weigh upon him.

Jacqueline is as much a hostage to the past as her husband. Born out of wedlock and orphaned in infancy by her mother's suicide, she too suffers the consequences of acute early deprivation. Both characters seek a realm in which they will enjoy the security denied them in childhood, and, unlike Yvonne and Geoffrey Firmin, the Llewelyns actually do enter the Columbian paradise. In the hamlet of Eridanus they acquire a two-room cabin, which is for them less a house than something to be worn "like a shell" (F80). There they come to feel at one with the rhythms of nature—the tides, the seasons, the life cycles of beasts and flowers. It strikes Ethan that "the very immediacy of the eternities by which they were surrounded and nursed...conspired on every hand to reassure and protect them" (F79). Unfortunately this *religio loci* also renders them vulnerable; the Harbor Board's threat to dispossess the Eridanus settlers seems to the Llewelyns beyond endurance. It is not just the destroyers and ingrates who face eviction, as in the *Volcano,* but those who want most desperately to preserve their Eden as well. Ethan and Jacqueline thus find themselves doubly burdened: they must cope with both the lingering effects of wretched childhoods and the bliss-turned-to-ashes of their recent past.

The pilgrimage to Gabriola Island in the Straits of Georgia represents an effort to renew their faith in life, to make the phoenix "clap its wings" (F90) once again. Lowry remarks, in a letter to Albert Erskine, that "the difficulty of the future taking any shape at all...is really the whole plot" of *October Ferry.*[30] At the same time, the Llewelyns' inability to trust in new possibilities accounts for there being so little present action in the book. Most of what happens on the bus traveling up the coast of Vancouver Island, in Nanaimo, and on the boat bound for Gabriola has no importance in its own right but merely furnishes a pretext for reflections on the past. Ostensibly the trip affords Ethan and Jacqueline a chance to liberate themselves from their "infantile fixation"[31] on Eridanus, whereas in fact it is an instance of regression: "by drawing close to Nanaimo in their journey northward they had also drawn so much closer to their old home that those very peaks and ravines of the mainland...now possessed the terrible familiarity of ancient landmarks to the heart" (F153). Gabriola itself is, both in its situation and character, nearer still to the existence they are supposedly relinquishing. On the map their route would, as Ethan realizes, describe a triangle, and in matters of the heart triangles constitute figures of ambivalence.

Authentic life does not lie in a second retreat on Gabriola comparable to the one in Eridanus. The latter has given Ethan a necessary respite from suffering, a compensation for the support lacking in his early experience, but he is no more free to exempt himself permanently from the human lot than Hans Castorp is to remain forever in the Berghof. Every retreat implies a corresponding advance, lest it result in a slackening of moral being. It is not at all clear what course Ethan should follow after leaving Eridanus, except that he must confront his anxiety if he is to have any prospect of attaining equilibrium. He seems to be making a start in that direction in "The Perilous Chapel" episode. Feeling himself an outcast from both his father's house and the one with which he has replaced it, the protagonist encounters a Roman Catholic priest aboard the Gabriola ferry and solicits his prayers. Ethan is not, he admits, a believer in any traditional sense nor has he been an especially steadfast seeker. "I can't explain. . .why I spoke to you," he tells the cleric, "I feel like a hypocrite. All I know is that I want passionately to *want* not to be a hypocrite!" (F304). This confession of spiritual poverty, together with the paternal reassurance that the priest offers, marks a shift in Ethan's attitude; he begins to construe occurrences—a Coleridgean albatross flying toward Gabriola, the solicitude of several passengers and crewmen for an ailing woman, the unexpected return of their ferry to Nanaimo—as signs that "we are not altogether unwatched" (F320). He is not ready to undertake a grand leap of faith, yet the rekindling of religious hope serves to buoy him up. "When 'divine judgment' is interpreted as a psychological complex and forgiveness as a remnant of the 'father-image,'" remarks Paul Tillich, "what once was the power in those symbols can still be present and create the courage to be in spite of the experience of an infinite gap between what we are and what we ought to be." This courage, he goes on to say, "is rooted in the God who appears when God has disappeared in the anxiety of doubt."[32] Tillich's conception of God as the ground of being is, of course, no more subject to verification than any other metaphysical proposition; nonetheless, it is a belief that may help to summon the very strength it posits. Lowry's protagonist craves just this sense that his existence has, its apparent futility notwithstanding, some warrant.

The Llewelyns learn, as the ferry sets out across the strait a second time, that the Eridanus squatters' eviction has been deferred indefinitely. Jacqueline takes the reprieve as a sign that they should return to their cabin. Ethan recognizes the undesirability of that course; he does not see, however, that settling on Gabriola would break the trajectory of their lives in much the same way. Neither, it appears, does the author perceive it. Lowry's attempt to fit *October Ferry* with the tonic resolution figured forth in that "deep, protracted chord of mournful triumph" (F332) which the boat sounds as it approaches the island seems contrived. The reader would, he hoped, perceive the silhouetted figures swinging lanterns and calling out across the water as indications that "Ethan is now being received by mankind" and conclude that "the characters journey toward their own recovery."[33] Unfortunately the symbols of this transformation are hollow, and the entire scene, which Lowry intended as a parallel to *Bergschluchten* in *Faust,* is in fact no more convincingly rendered than the end of *Dark as the Grave.* Although the last chapter, along with much of the rest of *October Ferry,* fails as art, it does offer a poignant reflection of the writer's dilemma while he was composing the book. Continuing to live on the beach at Dollarton and, at the same time, trying to become reconciled to the prospect of leaving it, he considered himself "on the one hand damned Ahab-wise in the midst of Paradise and on the other still mysteriously given the grace to live there even if it is only the privilege of great guilt."[34] One feels that, as with Berryman's persona in the *Dream Songs,* there must be a law against Malcolm Lowry and his protagonists.

October Ferry evolved from a short story written in 1946, and as late as 1953 Lowry continued to regard the work as essentially modest in scope: "it grew almost to a novel on its own," he reported to Harold Matson, "and is still not quite subdued and cut to size."[35] Had the author accomplished the promised redaction of *October Ferry* rather than enlarging it further, he might well have given us a version superior to the one we have been considering. Lowry's approach to writing was, he acknowledged, "subjective rather than objective, a better equipment... for a certain kind of poet than a novelist."[36] Given his predilection for the lyric rather than the dramatic mode, one might expect him to have found shorter forms of fiction more tractable than the novel, and indeed the most successful works of his last decade are those that range from fifteen to seventy pages in print. At the same time, one understands that the artist, having triumphed over his limitations in the *Volcano,* could not resign himself to doing short pieces exclusively. The stories he composed during the late 1940s and early 1950s were, in his eyes, "practice on a few smaller peaks"[37] for the more ambitious projects, the Popocatepetls, ahead. By 1951 he had come to think of these stories, initially designed for magazine publication, as parts of a single work, *Hear Us O Lord from Heaven Thy Dwelling Place,* and had begun attending consciously to the interrelations of theme, image, and setting essential to its integrity.

Lowry's plans for *Hear Us O Lord* proved nearly as protean as those he framed for the *Voyage* as a whole. The number of stories he meant to include grew from six in October 1951 to twelve by September 1952. Of the seven pieces that Margerie Lowry finally admitted to the volume four were drawn from the original roster: "Through the Panama," "Strange Comfort Afforded by the Profession," "Elephant and Colosseum," and "The Forest Path to the Spring."[38] The author had subsequently indicated, in a letter to Erskine, that "Present Estate of Pompeii" was to occupy the antepenultimate place in the collection.[39] His published correspondence does not specifically mention "The Bravest Boat" or "Gin and Goldenrod" in connection with *Hear Us O Lord,* but he does refer to the former independently on several occasions in ways that suggest his particular fondness for it.[40] One concludes, then, that Margerie Lowry has been generally faithful to her husband's intentions regarding the choice and disposition of the stories. She did, however, omit two whose inclusion he had proposed, "In the Black Hills" and "Ghostkeeper." Both have since appeared separately and been collected in the recent *Psalms and Songs,* which contains virtually the last publishable gleanings from the manuscripts in Vancouver. Before discussing *Hear Us O Lord* further, we ought perhaps to pause and consider these fugitives.

"Kristbjorg's Story: In the Black Hills" need not detain us for long. The tale is related by a Danish emigrant who is living out his days, we learn in "The Forest Path," as a fisherman in British Columbia and concerns an experience he has had as a young man in South Dakota. In the town of Deadwood, back in 1906, an anonymous German miner had seemed to find satisfaction or, at any rate, relief only by swiftly consuming enough whiskey to make himself lose consciousness. "Apparently," the narrator infers, "he wished to obliterate something."[41] Kristbjorg has no interest in the man's motives or identity—why should anybody care about matters the German himself wants to forget? The Dane is content to note that the miner keeps himself clean and pays for his own drinks. Hence he is "no bum" but rather a "bindle stiff," an itinerant worker who carries his belongings in a bundle. The incident on which the story hinges consists in Kristbjorg's discovering one summer day that the German has succumbed to alcoholic poisoning. Thereupon the patrons of Lent Morris's saloon, who have remained indifferent to the victim while he lived, collect sufficient funds to bury him in an unmarked grave on boot hill. In the course of his narration, the Dane celebrates such frontier virtues as generosity, tolerance (toward everyone but liars), lack of sentimentality, and personal freedom. "And maybe after all it was a glorious death," he concludes. "In those days a man could get away somewhere."[42] One recalls the Consul's pleas for noninterference in the affairs of others. Whether the author would finally have retained "In the

Black Hills" as a part of *Hear Us O Lord* is, of course, a moot question, and Margerie Lowry's decision to exclude the story is understandable enough. Although its themes are consonant with those of the collection as a whole, its style, a none too consistent attempt to capture a workingman's idiom, is out of key. In any case, the piece is very slight—scarcely more than an anecdote— and would have added nothing of importance to *Hear Us O Lord.*

"Ghostkeeper" is another matter. In all likelihood, Margerie Lowry elected to omit the story from *Hear Us O Lord* because it was among those unfinished works that resisted editorial polishing. That she eventually chose to publish it in unaltered form commends itself on grounds other than scholarly fastidiousness. Since what we have is evidently a first draft with memoranda for possible revisions, we find ourselves privy to Lowry's shaping of his material at a quite early stage of composition.[43] Like *October Ferry,* the piece draws much of its power from "the bloody agony of the writer writing." One symptom of his malaise was a block against putting pen to paper that obliged him to compose by dictating to his wife, a practice that conferred upon "Ghostkeeper" the kind of roughhewn immediacy one associates with oral narration.[44] The openness of its form derives as well from the author's attempt "to give the illusion of things—appearances, possibilities, ideas, even resolutions—in a state of perpetual metamorphosis," since, as he goes on to say, "life is indeed a sort of delirium" (P224). If this determination to render experience in all its protean complexity helps account for the many loose ends in "Ghostkeeper," it also explains why the tale conveys a richer sense of felt life than all but two or three of the pieces in *Hear Us O Lord.*

Like the initial story in that collection, "Ghostkeeper" begins with a walk through Stanley Park in Vancouver. The protagonist Tom Goodheart, an aspiring novelist, writes a newspaper column for which he is seeking topics as he strolls with his wife, Mary. Their appellations seem generic rather then personal: "his own name," reflects Tom, "[is] too much like Pilgrim's Progress"

(P219) to use in fiction. The Goodhearts are in fact stand-ins for the artist and his spouse; at times the names "Malc" and "Margie" appear in lieu of "Tom" and "Mary." On the surface the narrative moves among such occurrences as the discovery of a wrecked lifeboat with "H. Ghostkeeper" chalked on its bow, an encounter with children who throw stones at ducks, the viewing of a film set in New Brighton, England, Tom's birthplace, and the losing, finding, and exchange of watches, including one with "Henrik Ghostkeeper" engraved on it. On a deeper stratum the story consists in the protagonist's efforts to read the signatures of these events, at once banal and mysterious, and to make them cohere sufficiently that they can serve as the basis for a work of fiction. Goodheart labors under considerable tension: he is barely in touch with many of his own emotions, unsure of his craft, and without firm roots in any community. At one point Tom feels himself to be no more than "an old buttoned-up overcoat" (P212). Only his marriage helps secure his identity. In all these respects, he is, of course, fashioned in his creator's image.

Given Lowry's inclination to allow "Ghostkeeper" to reflect his anxieties as a writer, it follows that the piece will be more concerned with the process of its own construction than with the matter it ostensibly exists to relate. Above all, it underscores the baffling alternatives confronting the author: "no sooner did poor Goodheart come to some sort of decision as to what line his story should take than it was as if a voice said to him: 'But you see, you can't do it like that, that's not the meaning at all, or rather it's only one meaning—if you're going to get anywhere near the truth you'll have twenty different plots and a story no one will take'" (P219). What, Tom asks himself, can one do with a narrative in which the dominant symbol, the watch—connected with, among other things, the sense of loss, blindness, expatriation, the need for money, generosity, guilt, the curse of the name Ghostkeeper, justice, compassion, the death of a king, Ezekiel's wheels within wheels, and a time out of joint—lacks even a "consistent ambiguity?" Under such conditions, the narrator can hardly be expected to conclude the tale by drawing all the threads together; he can only end it "in a manner not remotely suggested by its beginning or indeed having very much to do with it" (P225). By dramatizing his problems as a storyteller, Lowry manages to convert liabilities into assets. The main importance of "Ghostkeeper" lies in its exposure of false bottoms in our conventional modes of understanding. At least in this regard, it calls to mind the much more elegant metafictions of Nabokov and Borges.

Hear Us O Lord from Heaven Thy Dwelling Place was, Lowry told his editor, "shaping up less like an ordinary book of tales than a sort of novel of an odd aeolian kind."[45] If the collection constitutes a novel, it is indeed a peculiar one, for the seven stories that were finally included have no more action or character development than the two we have just considered. The protagonists, artists and seafarers who can be distinguished from one another only by their names and superficial differences in their personal histories, are all transparent masks for the author. His term "aeolian" indicates the essential nature of the book much more accurately than "novel" does: the pieces are more nearly akin to meditative-descriptive lyrics than they are to traditional narrative modes, and Lowry hoped that they would make a "beautiful sound when taken together."[46] Read in sequence, even though the order in which they appear does not correspond precisely to his design, they do form what might fairly be described as a symphonic prose poem. *Hear Us O Lord* begins with an exposition of the Eridanus theme, followed immediately by a movement away from the idyllic life on Burrard Inlet, across tempestuous seas, to the dissolution represented in the three stories with Italian settings. In the last two pieces, the reprise, we return to the northern paradise, the enjoyment of which is qualified, however, by the threat of eviction. The overall structure thus recapitulates the cyclical rhythms everywhere present in the vistas of forest and sea that serve as the tonic chord of the collection.[47]

He opens the first story, "The Bravest Boat," with a full-page evocation of scene that contrasts the natural beauty of British

Columbia with the sordidness of Vancouver, called in this instance Enochvilleport. His idiom, rich in images of purification, renders the landscape almost animate:

> It was a day of spindrift and blowing sea-foam, with black clouds presaging rain driven over the mountains from the sea by a wild March wind.
> But a clean silver sea light came from along the horizon.
> ... And far away over in America the snowy volcanic peak of Mount Hood stood on high, disembodied, cut off from earth, yet much too close, which was an even surer presage of rain, as though the mountains had advanced, or were advancing. (H13)

Against this backdrop of vitality are set the red cedars in Stanley Park, "dying rather than live longer near civilization" (H13). It is a civilization that finds its vulgarity epitomized in the hamburger stand and its rapacity in the sawmill, a Moloch devouring the wilderness. Man's estrangement from the earth is in fact the major theme not just of this story but of the entire collection.

The soullessness of Enochvilleport is redeemed only by the presence of a few squatters' shacks, structures "that might have been driven out of the city altogether, down to the water's edge into the sea itself, where they stood on piles, like fishermen's huts (which several of them apparently were), or on rollers, some dark and tumbledown, others freshly and prettily painted, these last quite evidently built or placed with some human need for beauty in mind, even if under the permanent threat of eviction" (H17). The little community, which remains unnamed in this story, is of course Eridanus. All the tales except "Strange Comfort Afforded by the Profession" and "Elephant and Colosseum" either depict life in that hamlet or use it as a yardstick to evaluate the spirit of other places.

More than a page of "The Bravest Boat" passes before the author peoples the scene, and then only with figures as diminutive as those in a Chinese landscape painting. The story is half over before these characters are particularized enough even to have names. Sigurd and Astrid Storlesen, "two good people" who find happiness in the life of wild things, are married lovers, he fifteen years older than she. Their peripatetic dialogues about her discovery of a toy boat bearing a message from Sigurd—Lowry's *bateau ivre*—and their imaginative reconstruction of its twelve-year peregrination constitute the main "action" of the piece. That "The Bravest Boat" is more a lyric meditation than a short story limits the seriousness of such defects as wooden dialogue and shallow characterization without altogether excusing them. One does not feel the absence of action in the traditional sense as a flaw, however, for the Storlesens' attitude of wise passiveness toward the natural scene that plays over and purifies their sensibilities is essential to the emergence of Lowry's theme. Sigurd owes his youthful appearance and energy to the regenerative powers of his young wife, and their relationship thus takes its place in the process they behold everywhere about them. The true protagonist of "The Bravest Boat" is, as Dylan Thomas phrases it, "the force that drives the water through the rocks."[48]

As the tale draws to a close, the couple walk along the beach strewn with the "macabre fruit of the sea," detritus cast up by the March tides. In the midst of this desolation, they experience a moment of epiphany, a reverent intuition "that all this with its feeling of death and destruction and barrenness was only an appearance, that beneath the flotsam...existed, just as in the forest, a stirring and stretching of life, a seething of spring" (H26). Theme and imagery form an intimate connection between "The Bravest Boat" and the last piece in the collection, "The Forest Path to the Spring." Together the two stories provide a frame of affirmation, an enchanted circle, within which the fears and threats that rack the protagonists of the intervening tales may be contained.

The story of the little boat's storm-tossed wanderings is followed by the fictionalized record of an actual voyage from Vancouver to Rotterdam that royalties from *Under the Volcano* enabled the Lowrys to take late in 1947, "Through the Panama" has as its subtitle "From the Journal of Sigbjørn Wilderness," and its form is indeed that of a journal, a notebook full of un-mortared *aperçus* designed to show the writer's mind at work molding experience into art. In its intent, then, the piece re-sembles "Ghostkeeper." Lowry confronts us in "Panama" with a bizarre assortment of autobiographical reminiscences, descrip-tions of scenery, ship's noises, observations on the state of mod-ern literature, weather reports, political opinions, encomia to French seamanship and cuisine, poems, ornithological inven-tories, prospectuses for novels, newspaper clippings, immigration forms in two languages, and marginal glosses from *The Rime of the Ancient Mariner* and a history of the Canal Zone.[49] No reader of the *Volcano*, where the author manages to dramatize menus, will dispute the possibility of his turning such materials to literary account, and indeed "Through the Panama" does offer much to inform and delight the Lowry *aficionado*. The comparative art-lessness of the form appears to have given the novelist a welcome respite from the stringent demands he habitually made upon himself. At the same time, the work contains a good deal of mere abreaction, the kind of self-expression that, however therapeutic it may have been for Lowry, cannot produce the sort of resonance in our minds that it did in his. In a letter written in the summer of 1953, the author speaks of the need to "get some of the nonsense out of 'Through the Panama.' "[50] That many of its elements re-main undeveloped and unintegrated suggests that the projected revision never took place.

"Panama" is, then, more impressive in some of its parts than it is as a whole. Those that matter most concern the distinctive problems Lowry as a writer faced, and chief among these was, as we have seen, his inability to render convincingly characters who were not mirror images of himself. His persona Wilderness claims that he is, "unlike most artists, a true human being." Un-fortunately what Sigbjørn means is *menschlich, allzumenschlich,* for he goes on to explain that "this is the way the majority of human beings see other human beings, as shadows, themselves the only reality" (H85).

Narcissism, the "insatiable albatross" that hangs around the author's neck, accounts for his lack of distance from his characters. Indeed he makes the predicament of "the double, the triple, the quadruple 'I' " (H73) a major theme of "Panama." The diarist Wilderness has become enmeshed in the plot of a novel he is working on, *Dark as the Grave,* whose protagonist Martin Trumbaugh[51] is himself entangled in a book he has written. This latter work is *Under the Volcano,* referred to in the journal as *The Valley of the Shadow of Death,* where we witness the Consul in turn identifying with the Massachusetts pioneer William Blackstone. Sigbjørn frequently makes unannounced shifts from his "own" mind to that of his character Martin, leaving us uncertain whose point of view is being represented. What Lowry actually offers us in these sections of "Panama" is a cross-examination of his extraordinarily involuted consciousness, and it is in such interior dialogues that his prose becomes most intensely alive. His strategy recalls the mirrors within mirrors of *Les faux-monnayeurs,* although it would be unfair to Lowry to press a comparison between his unfinished narrative and Gide's brilliantly realized novel.

The artist's involvement with his creations often leads to blurred distinctions between the fictional and the actual. As the ship sails down the Mexican coast, Wilderness speculates on the power of the word: *"Dark as the Grave is about the death of Fernando, who is Dr. Vigil in The Valley of the Shadow. Real* death that is, we discovered.... *The Valley of the Shadow* worked like an infernal machine. Dr. Vigil is dead like the Consul.... No wonder my letters were returned" (H36). As we have observed, Lowry lived in order to incorporate his experiences in literature and his most vivid experience was the act of writing itself. For Proust and Mallarmé this circumflexion turned into the most fecund of themes. For Lowry it proved fatal. The life the writer embodied in his art crystalized into an alien self bent upon annihilating him, for he became his own work, and his identity apart from it withered. The handful of sleeping tablets the novelist devoured on the night of 27 June 1957 was only a ratification of the suicide he had been committing by degrees for many years. "My faithful general Phenobarbus, treacherous to the last? (Note for Martin.)" (H48), writes Sigbjørn in his journal.

Lowry's claim that "Through the Panama" parallels Fitzgerald's *Crack-Up,* except that "instead of cracking the protagonist's fission begins to be healed,"[52] seems wishful thinking. Wilderness's alleged recovery consists in his weathering a patently symbolic, poorly rendered North Atlantic storm and in his discovering, once again, how to pray. What the preceding sixty pages have revealed about his psychic condition does not, however, lead to an optimistic prognosis. And indeed the Sigbjørn we meet in the next story, "Strange Comfort Afforded by the Profession," has suffered a relapse.[53] He languishes in Rome, trying to find material for his fiction in stichometrical sets of notes taken in the house where Keats died and in the Poe shrine in Richmond.

The obsessions that rule him in "Through the Panama"—the problem of identity, drink, the magic of words, and the drift toward death—have lost none of their force. "Sigbjørn Wilderness!" he muses. "The very sound of his name was like a bellbuoy—or more euphoniously a light-ship—broken adrift, and washing in from the Atlantic on a reef. Yet how he hated to write it down (loved to see it in print?)—though like so much else with him it had little reality unless he did" (H102). He avoids signing the guest book in the Keats museum both because of his primitive fear that externalizing a part of his selfhood will increase his vulnerability and because he cannot afford to extend in any way his identification with an artist whose self-destructive tendencies threaten to reinforce his own. In his notebook Sigbjørn copies a letter from the painter Joseph Severn that recounts Keats's renunciation of any hope for a further career: "he says the continued stretch of his imagination has already killed him and were he

to recover he would not write another line" (H101). It is not difficult to envision the terror these words evoke in a writer troubled
by the suspicion that his talent has been exhausted. The reason
Wilderness flees from the "comforting darkness" of the poet's
house to the haven of a bar is plain enough. He too is "half in love
with easeful Death."

As Sigbjørn reviews his observations on Keats, he comes across
remarks written in the same notebook during a visit to the Valen-
tine Museum two years before. Among them is a quotation from
one of Poe's letters that echoes the despair voiced by the dying
Keats. Sigbjørn's reaction to Poe's cry from the depths offers a
fine illustration of the ironic, reflexive consciousness he shares
with the two poets:

> The sensation produced by reading these notes was really very
> curious. First, he was conscious of himself reading them here
> in this Roman bar, then of himself in the Valentine Museum
> in Richmond, Virginia, reading the letters through the glass
> case and copying fragments from these down, then of poor
> Poe sitting blackly somewhere writing them. Beyond this
> was the vision of Poe's foster father likewise reading some of
> these letters, for all he knew unheedingly, yet solemnly put-
> ting them away for what turned out to be posterity, these
> letters which, whatever they might not be, were certainly—
> he thought again—intended to be private. But were they
> indeed? Even here at this extremity Poe must have felt that
> he was transcribing the story that was E. A. Poe, at this very
> moment of what he conceived to be his greatest need, his
> final—however consciously engineered—disgrace, felt a
> certain reluctance, perhaps, to send what he wrote, as if he
> were thinking: Damn it, I could use some of that, it may not
> be so hot, but it is at least too good to waste on my foster
> father. (H106–7)

The disposition to cannibalize experience, the Mallarméan
stance that everything exists *pour aboutir à un livre,* is evident in
Lowry's own correspondence, which contains phrases and relates

occurrences that crop up again in his fiction. In a 1940 letter to Conrad Aiken, the writer describes the atrocious conditions under which he has been living in Vancouver, "the most hopeless of all cities of the lost," and expresses the fear that he is on the verge of a mental collapse, "though cheerfulness is always breaking in."[54] Toward the end of "Strange Comfort" Wilderness discovers in another of his notebooks the draft of an old letter, wry and poignant in the manner of the author's entreaty to Aiken, but directed to a much less understanding parental surrogate, the lawyer his father has appointed to supervise the son's finances. This fictional epistle has been written, in parallel circumstances, from Seattle, a "damnable place with the highest suicide rate in the Union" (H112). The forgotten misery the letter recalls joins with Sigbjørn's present anxiety and causes him to break off reading. He then proceeds to cross his words out, line by line, as though he could thereby cancel the burden of memory. At the same time he begins to regret the action, "for now, damn it, he wouldn't be able to use it" (H112). Ultimately Wilderness cannot elude the "Demon of severe response"[55] that pursued Keats and Poe, the lyric impulse that battens on its host. Nor does he truly desire to escape. The dignity conferred by suffering for his vocation as the poets have done is an austere but sufficient compensation.

Although "Strange Comfort Afforded by the Profession" is less ambitious in conception than "Through the Panama," it constitutes a more adept and moving evocation of the writer's predicament than the longer narrative. For one thing the note-taking theme that runs through the two stories acquires more point in the second where it is combined with the recovery of *temps perdu.* And for another Lowry's juxtaposition of his protagonist with two artists whose heroism and pathos have almost legendary significance for us lends a richness to his characterization of Sigbjørn that is absent in "Panama." After the virtuosity of "Strange Comfort," the next two stories, "Elephant and Colosseum" and "Present Estate of Pompeii," are acute disappointments.

The hero of the fourth story in the collection bears another of Lowry's fanciful appellations, Kennish Drumgold Cosnahan. "Elephant and Colosseum" opens with Cosnahan sipping a glass of milk in a Via Veneto café, trying to recover from a spiritual hangover induced by the publication of a novel resembling *Ultramarine*. This story is Lowry's most sustained exploration of the hazards of literary success—the movie options that come to nothing, the preoccupation with reviewers' verdicts, and above all the difficulty of severing oneself from the published work and starting anew. The flaw that garrotes "Elephant and Colosseum" is, once again, the author's failure to bring his protagonist sufficiently to life for us to believe in him or care very much about his problems. During his last years in British Columbia, the artist withdrew into an isolation so profound that he became progressively less capable of defining his characters in terms of a social matrix. *Under the Volcano* is hardly a novel of manners, but the common life of Quauhnahuac that serves as a backdrop to the Consul's agony has at least been sensitively observed and vividly represented. The Rome through which Cosnahan wanders is, in comparison, etiolated.[56]

Drumgold's encounter with the alien city so unnerves him that he ends by taking refuge in the Borghese zoo where, opposite the elephant cages, his "somber panic" finally yields to the warmth of animistic revery: "Like the sacred ibis who has the habit of standing on one leg for hours at a time by the Nile, in a manner which can only strike most human beings as idiotic, so in its state of deep abstraction, with the elephant. . . . Who are we to say that the elephant does not have some higher comprehension of the will, as do the great mystics who inhabit some of the regions whence they come?" (H163). Lowry meant the tale to be comic, and indeed a gentle humor, of which the preceding quotation is a fair sample, does inform a number of passages; but the hopeful resolution—Cosnahan's determination to go back to America and begin writing again—is not particularly convincing. "Elephant and Colosseum" may be more buoyant in tone than the two stories that precede it, but at bottom it too rests on "caryatids of human anguish" (H172).

"Present Estate of Pompeii" takes place under yet another volcano. The protagonist Roderick Fairhaven's fear of the "noisome and shattered abyss" (H186) at the core of Vesuvius recalls Geoffrey Firmin's sense that he is falling into the crater of Popocatepetl, as the *sinarquistas* cast him into the barranca at the close of the *Volcano*. Through the ministrations of a sympathetic wife, Fairhaven's malaise is rendered less severe than the Consul's; he merely *hears* his "real life plunging to its doom" (H177) and does not find himself compelled to act out the catastrophe.

In outward appearance the hero of "Present Estate of Pompeii" is modeled on Lowry's friend Downie Kirk, a Vancouver language teacher, but the reader soon perceives that Roderick is in fact another of the author's pasteboard masks. As in the case of Drumgold Cosnahan, his portrait turns out a *nature morte*. Indeed the entire account of the tour through the ruins, with its flat dialogue and forced wit, is stillborn. Nearly all the energized writing in the piece occurs when Lowry abandons travel impressions and has the protagonist muse on his home in Eridanus, with its forest paths, cold pure sea, and mountains rising through turquoise haze. In these dithyrambic meditations Fairhaven recaptures the feeling of oneness with the earth he so desperately misses in Europe. At times the natural scene he evokes succeeds, through the power of its beauty, in making even the incursions of technology seem rich and strange: "Now over the water," he recalls, "came the slow warning bell of a freight train chiming on the rail over Port Boden as for a continual vespers, now closer, now receding, now Byzantine in its timbre, as it vibrated in the water, now dolorous like Oaxaquenian bells, now a blue sound, now as it approached, fuller, more globular, then fading, but always as if some country sound heard long ago that might have inspired a Wordsworth or a Coleridge to describe church bells borne over the fields to some wandering lovers at evening" (H193). But the effects of civilization rarely occasion such lyric moments. The pillar of smoke that obscures the sky when the tanker *Salinas* catches fire across the inlet from Eridanus forms an ominous parallel to the threatening summit of Vesuvius, with the crucial difference that in the shadow of the volcano nature menaces society whereas in British Columbia the reverse holds true.[57] Ultimately the consequences may be much the same, Lowry implies, except that the Canadians will not find their ruins worth preserving.

Fairhaven's parenthetic reflections on Eridanus look back to "The Bravest Boat" and forward to the last two stories in *Hear Us O Lord,* which are immediately concerned with life in the woods. The protagonists of "Gin and Goldenrod," the Wildernesses, have Canada's history of spoliation very much in mind, for the "suburban dementia" of tract housing now extends almost to their doorstep. Of the wild creatures they were accustomed to seeing in the forest, only a solitary garter snake remains, and it too wriggles away as the couple walk down their path. The lost-paradise theme is quickly rendered explicit: "Ruination and vulgarization had become a habit," Sigbjørn observes. "They had found a sort of peace, a sort of heaven, and were now losing it again" (H204). The threat to their happiness has, Wilderness indicates, led him to seek alcoholic consolation, although he himself recognizes that this explanation for his drinking oversimplifies the matter. The principal action of "Gin and Goldenrod" consists in husband and wife's seeking out a local bootlegger in order to settle a debt Sigbjørn has acquired through misplaced generosity: like a latter-day William Blackstone, he has stood a band of Indians to a Sunday evening *dégustation* of firewater. Even the remorse he feels en route to the bootlegger's cannot keep him from responding to "the beacon, the pharos, of the possible drink" (H210) when he arrives there. The metaphor echoes the name of the Consul's favorite cantina, the Farolito, and indeed Wilderness's trek along the path marked *To Dark Rosslyn* does constitute a comic reprise of Geoffrey's journey through the dark wood in which the signs point *A Parián.* As in "Present Estate of

Pompeii," a wife ready to mother her spouse helps make the difference. The tale ends with the couple's spirits revived and the promise of conciliatory martinis at home. When one considers the role alcohol has played in the story, he may well have some doubts about the "hope [that begins] to bloom again" (H214) for the Wildernesses; nevertheless, it is plain that the artist meant to represent their homecoming as a victory of sorts. "Gin and Goldenrod" is a slight but, in its own terms, successful piece. Its strength resides in its simple, effective plot and the passion with which Lowry develops the implications that a laying waste of the Canadian Eden has for those who love it and one another.

Midway through the composition of *Under the Volcano,* ensnared in its rococo intricacies, the author declared his preference for a fiction "bald and winnowed, like Sibelius."[58] One can hardly describe the style of Lowry's later writings as spare, but the stories in *Hear Us O Lord* do evince his desire for a chastening of form. This aspiration he realized most fully in "The Forest Path to the Spring," an amalgam of lyric meditation, evocation of natural scene, and narrative, with the emphasis even more distinctly on the first two elements than it is elsewhere in the collection. Perhaps one can most aptly characterize "The Forest Path," like the hymn sung by the fisherfolk of Eridanus, as "a poem of God's mercy" (H222). It is fiction only to the extent that Lowry selects and alters details of his personal history to fit a design, in much the way that Thoreau telescopes the time he spent at Walden to accord with the cycle of the seasons. The author drops his masks and tells the story in the first person.

As he walks along the forest path, the narrator likens himself to a "priest pacing in the aisles of a great cathedral at dusk" (H251), an analogy that points to the devotional impulse underlying the novella. He chants his litany in a Baudelairean temple whose living pillars

> Laissent parfois sortir de confuses paroles;
> L'homme y passe à travers des forêts de symboles
> Qui l'observent avec des regards familiers.[59]

Lowry employs the cathedral as a metaphor for the realm of natural correspondences at a number of points in "The Forest Path." Indeed it appears first on the opening page: "Often all you could see in the whole world of the dawn was a huge sun with two pines silhouetted in it, like a great blaze behind a Gothic cathedral" (H215–16). In the *Volcano* Jacques Laruelle longs for the elevation and grace of Chartres but recognizes that the integration it represents is beyond his reach. The churrigueresque sinuosity of Taxco cathedral comes closer to figuring forth the actuality of his and the Firmins' lives. For the inhabitants of Eridanus, on the other hand, Gothic splendor manifests itself every day in the radiance that quickens the earth.

The vital power that Lowry wished his art to serve makes itself felt most strongly in the movement of the inlet, "as mysterious and multiform in its motion and being, and in the mind as the mind flowed with it, as was that other Eridanus, the constellation in the heavens, the starry river in the sky, whose source only was visible to us, and visible reflected in the inlet too on still nights with a high brimming tide, before it curved away...round the Scepter of Brandenburg" (H234). Tide, stars, and mind harmonize in a chord, then sink into stillness, the stillness of the changeless Tao, the mother of all things.[60] One autumn day as the hero and his wife row across the inlet, the towering Cascades, mirrored in the water, seem to move along with them, like the pinnacle that strides after the author of *The Prelude*. The peaks that follow the couple on that occasion appear tutelary, but at other times the appalling chinook drives these same mountains "wild with chaos." At such moments the seagulls' angelic wings turn a "maniacal white." Wordsworth, similarly rent by the duplexity of nature, holds that "the sweet breath of heaven" and the tempest may join to "bring with them vernal promises."[61] The narrator of "The Forest Path" infers this promise from the "brilliant incessant water reflections and incandescence of light" that fill his house, indications that "soon the world would start rolling through the mountainous seas of winter toward inevitable spring"

(H242). On the artist falls the responsibility for discovering forms that will do justice to this majestic round.

Lowry's protagonist willingly undertakes the search but finds himself blocked by the very richness of his theme. He attempts both musical and literary renditions of it and finally resorts, when perplexity overwhelms him, to invocations of the heavenly muse. At one point he encounters the following petition, written years earlier over an unfinished score: "Dear Lord God, I earnestly pray you to help me order this work, ugly chaotic and sinful though it may be, in a manner that is acceptable in Thy sight. . . . It must be tumultuous, stormy, full of thunder, the exhilarating Word . . . must sound through it, pronouncing hope for man, yet it must also be balanced, grave, full of tenderness and compassion and humor" (H266). One cannot help remembering the Consul's plea for release from the "dreadful tyranny of self" (V289); but far from ending in futility as that supplication does, the prayer in "The Forest Path" is at least in part answered, that answer being the novella itself.

The masters of the American renaissance characteristically saw this continent as a prospective setting for paradise regained. Melville distills the yearning into a phrase when he speaks of "that unfallen, western world, which . . . revived the glories of those primeval times when Adam walked majestic as a God."[62] Most exponents of the North American Eden make it a man's province. Lowry, on the other hand, imagines a "stalwart Columbian Adam, who [has] calmly stolen back with his Eve into Paradise" (H24). Marriage was for him a prime mode of integration, a stay against a centrifugal world. One thinks of the inscription on Laruelle's tower: *No se puede vivir sin amar.* And indeed no one lives in Eridanus who does not love. The narrator's wife in "The Forest Path" nurses her husband back to health and helps attune him to the rhythm of their surroundings. "I reflected how little I had known of the depths and tides of a woman until now," he writes, underscoring a link with the maternal sea. "Often I had the feeling that she had some mysterious correspondence with all nature around her unknown to me, and I thought that perhaps she was herself the eidolon of everything we loved in Eridanus" (H247). She seems at times more eidolon than realized personage. One can, in this instance, defend Lowry's idealization of his heroine as essential to the part she plays, that of a Beatrice leading her man to the summit of consciousness.

She performs this role not merely by teaching him about seabirds, wildflowers, and constellations but even more by serving as a medium through which he can experience the world anew, in innocence and love. One evening as her husband is returning through the forest she rushes to welcome him, and a surge of tenderness overwhelms them both. "Just for an instant," the narrator remembers,

> I felt that had she not come down the path to meet me, I might indeed have disappeared, to spend the rest of my extraterritorial existence searching for her in some limbo.
> . . . And over my wife's shoulder, coming across the inlet toward the lighthouse, I saw a deer swimming.
> This reminded me that despite the wind it was warm enough for me to start swimming again. . . so I went straight in, and it was as though I had been baptized afresh. (H270)

Like Thoreau's morning swims in Walden Pond, plunges into an amniotic bath from which a man emerges reborn, this exercise is religious and one of the best things Lowry's protagonist does.

If the hero's wife recalls Beatrice, then on at least one occasion, the dreamlike encounter with the mountain lion, he himself resembles Dante, whose path is similarly blocked in Canto I of the *Inferno*. [63] When the narrator calmly orders the cat to be gone, it slinks guiltily away into the dark forest, leaving him to his less than tranquil thoughts: "it was as though I had actually been on the lookout for something on the path that had seemed ready, on every side, to spring out of our paradise at us, that was nothing so much as the embodiment in some frightful animal form of those nameless somnambulisms, guilts, ghouls of past delirium, wounds to other souls and lives ready to leap out and destroy me, to destroy us, and our happiness" (H263-64). It is his possession by these and other past selves, splinters of his true being, that holds the narrator of "The Forest Path" in thrall. History lies as heavily on him as it does on the Indian in chapter 9 of the *Volcano* who carries his father on his back or on the Ahab who compares himself to Adam, "staggering beneath the piled centuries since Paradise."[64] "The Forest Path" recounts its hero's struggle to free himself or, at any rate, to shift the burden so that it might be borne with less suffering.

Melville read in Hawthorne's "Young Goodman Brown" and "Earth's Holocaust" a lesson that changed the course of his art. *Moby-Dick* differs from the South Sea romances that precede it in recognizing that the human heart itself engenders the corruption of Eden.[65] One need not suppose that Lowry derived this insight from Melville to perceive the kinship between his lion and the white whale, for the significance of the beasts may be understood only if we look into the somber depths of the men who confront them. In their souls we discover a "ferocious destructive ignorance" that is the exact counterpart of "the avenging, man-hating spirit of the wilderness" (H243) known to the Indians of British Columbia as the Wendigo. The characteristic means by which this dreadful force expresses itself are the forest fire and suicide. Once as the narrator walks to the spring he finds a frayed, but still strong, rope lying like a serpent on the path. "Had I actually been tempted to kill myself?" (H260) he asks, aghast at the thought.

Possession by demons representing the past or the chaotic elements in nature is a major threat to human happiness, but the surest way to destroy it is to become possessive oneself. Men lose paradise in Lowry's world by trying to assume title to it. "Perhaps Adam was the first property owner and God, the first agrarian, ...kicked him out," speculates the Consul in one of his antic discourses, "for it's obvious to everyone these days...that the original sin was to be an owner of property" (V133). The primal offense consists, then, in usurping lordship of the earth and wreaking changes on it that violate its providential design. Like his author, Geoffrey Firmin retains the marks of a stern Wesleyan education, with the sermons on stewardship inflicted on him as a boy recast in a spirit of radical seriousness the homilist could never have anticipated. It is not hard to see why Lowry felt an affinity with Faulkner, whose protagonist in "The Bear" decries the division into "oblongs and squares" of an earth given man to hold "intact in the communal anonymity of brotherhood."[66] The cougar on the path stands, as Old Ben does, against the desecration of nature and the consequent profanation of humanity. "Who can be surprised," asks the narrator of "The Forest Path," "that the very elements, harnessed only for the earth's ruination and man's greed" (H240), should array themselves against him? As the Consul perceives, we must follow the example of William Blackstone and make our peace with the values of the Indians, men who knew how to live with the land, slain by the thousands in the conquest of the Americas. And still being slain, as the Indian dying by the roadside in the *Volcano* bears witness.

There are times in "The Forest Path" when the narrator finds himself tyrannized not only by the past but by the future as well. Eridanus is "a condemned community, perpetually under the shadow of eviction" (H225) cast by those who would replace the squatters' shacks with motels and subdivisions. Once again the evil of possession confronts him, and this time he finds its seat in his own soul. The couple come to Eridanus as honeymooners, not expecting to stay, and the fear of expulsion becomes acute only when they are tempted to think of the place as *theirs,* when they forget that it is an Eden partly because they have lived there provisionally. Happiness comes to them in moments valued for their own sake, moments they enjoy in a spirit of freedom, knowing that sooner or later the things which engender them must be relinquished, if possible without regret. The narrator and his wife experience their greatest triumph a few weeks after their house has burned, when, as he says, "careless of its charred and tragic smell we wonderfully picnicked within it, diving off the blackened posts into the natural swimming pool of our old living room and frightening away I have no doubt the devil himself,...the enemy of all humor in the face of disaster" (H280). Even the Consul, who does not hesitate to immerse himself in the destructive element, would find it difficult to surpass such buoyancy.

The path along which the protagonist goes through the woods to the spring serves as an Edenic alternative to the one that leads to Parián and mescal-saturated despair. As Thoreau was fond of remarking, there is no beverage more intoxicating than water to a man whose spirits are naturally high. "The Forest Path" resembles *Walden* in its determination "to front only the essential facts of life,"[67] especially those laid down by the elemental rhythms within and about us. In one crucial respect, however, the two writers and their works diverge: although Thoreau traveled much in Concord, there is little indication that he ever traversed hell. Lowry's spring may be a "joyous little stream" just before it enters the sea, but it still retains a faint tang of mushrooms and dead leaves from the somber woods and caverns through which it has passed. En route to the source the narrator sees, "through the trees, range beyond celestial range" (H215) of snowy peaks. If this sublime prospect suggests the possibility of transcendence, it also, we are not permitted to forget, embraces the things surmounted. Popocatepetl is snow-capped too and no less a part of "the great Cordilleras that [rib] the continent" (H229) than the heavenly Cascades. Plainly "The Forest Path" was designed to be a testament of hope, but it is a hope that can be realized only through a precarious balance of antinomies.

Lowry meant *Hear Us O Lord* to be a kind of "*Volcano* in reverse,"[68] and indeed the tragic vision of his masterwork and the comic spirit of "The Forest Path" do ultimately come together, with the hero of the latter enjoying the rebirth that eludes Geoffrey Firmin. It seems fitting that the artist should have conceived the final scene of the novella, which celebrates the coincidence of opposites, as a coda for the entire *Voyage that Never Ends.* [69] The journey on which Lowry was embarked, a passage undertaken by many poets and seers before him, involves a dying away of the old self into a more authentic mode of being where one discovers the myth he must render into life. "Stirb und werde!" as Goethe has it: until one heeds that injunction he remains no more than "ein trüber Gast / Auf der dunklen Erde."[70] That the novelist left most segments of the *Voyage* incomplete and that, in the end, he sank into oblivion in as dingy a fashion as his Consul does not invalidate the quest. As Firmin predicts, one finds in the catastrophe that awaits him "a certain element of triumph" (V139). On one level this triumph resides in the attitude of tragic gaiety with which he fares toward his death, but it is rooted finally in his power of vision. In dreams the Consul has seen a way through the abyss of self-absorption and beyond it a paradise of healing love; however dim that illumination may at times grow, it is never altogether quenched: he discerns in the void itself "the all-but-unretraceable path of God's lightning back to God" (V39). The route Geoffrey takes through the Inferno, could he but pursue it far enough, might turn into another, albeit the most roundabout, of those "twenty-one paths that lead back to Eden" (H269). In the artifice of eternity the forest trails to the barranca and to the spring converge.

Appendix

A Note on
Lowry Scholarship

The most complete bibliography of Lowry's writings is that of Earle Birney and Margerie Lowry in *Canadian Literature* 8 (spring 1961): 81–88, with supplements in issues 11 (winter 1962): 90–93 and 19 (winter 1964): 83–86. An updated list of Lowry's major publications appears in William H. New's *Malcolm Lowry: A Reference Guide* (Boston: G. K. Hall, 1978), together with a comprehensive bibliography of writings about Lowry through 1976. Although the amount of annotation New gives each item does not always reflect its relative importance, his guide is, nonetheless, indispensable to the student who wishes to investigate the large body of periodical literature on Lowry. I shall limit myself here to a brief survey of books dealing with the novelist's life and art.

Unquestionably the most significant piece of scholarship to emerge is Douglas Day's *Malcolm Lowry* (New York: Oxford Univ. Press, 1973). Day's biography is unlikely to be superseded in its rendering of such phases of the artist's experience as his crucial sojourn in Mexico (1936–38) or the voyage, three sheets to the wind, toward death following his departure from Canada in 1954. It is comparatively thin in its treatment of Lowry's life prior to his self-imposed exile from England and less thorough than it might have been in its depiction of the years in British Columbia. Scenes of dissipation and folly are recounted with a verve reminiscent of John Malcolm Brinnin on Dylan Thomas, while the writer's virtues are less vividly represented. Although the emphasis falls on interpreting the man rather than his fiction, the book does contain a good deal of criticism. The twenty-five pages Day gives to a direct consideration of the structure and themes of *Under the Volcano* are full of good sense—especially his insights into its religious dimension—but they are only prolegomena to the *Gestalt* critique of the novel that he proposes. He is severe in his judgment of all the later works apart from "The Forest Path to the Spring" and "Through the Panama." The large question Day leaves unanswered is how the man he portrays was able to pull himself together over the course of a decade and produce his masterpiece. (For a fuller discussion of Day, see my review in *Modern Philology* 74 [1976]: 218–21.)

One of the most vexing problems regarding the *Volcano* is the fact that, as Andrew Pottinger correctly observes, "the majority of . . . critics have directed their attention away from . . . [its] psychological or 'literal' level, and the consequent emphasis on symbolic and mythic interpretation has seriously dehumanized the novel" ("The Consul's 'Murder,' " *Canadian Literature* 67 [winter 1976]: 53). Perle Epstein's *The Private Labyrinth of Malcolm Lowry* (New York: Holt, Rinehart, and Winston, 1969) is a prime instance of this trend. She offers a reading of the *Volcano* in terms of the author's idiosyncratic cabalism, a tack she pursues so single-mindedly that it leads her into procrustean allegorizing. In an early review of the novel, Mark Schorer rightly declared that its form is capable of "holding event and symbol, story and meaning absolutely together, of preventing, that is, allegory" ("The Downward Flight of a Soul," *New York Herald Tribune Weekly Book Review,* 23 February 1947, p. 2). It may be that the exegesis of symbolist works always inclines toward allegory; nevertheless, it seems to me that the critic's duty is to resist this tendency and to remain faithful to the complexity of the artist's vision.

Kristofer Dorosz, in *Malcolm Lowry's Infernal Paradise* (Uppsala: Acta Universitatis Upsaliensis, 1976), takes a more balanced view of the cabalistic strain in the novel than does Epstein, seeing it as one of many elements in the protagonist's demonic inversion of hell and Elysium. The *Volcano* suffers, he declares, from a profusion of ambiguous detail that blurs its contours. This difficulty stems, I think, from Dorosz's tendency to concentrate on symbolic motifs and to disregard the dramatic context that gives definition to them. David Markson contends, in *Malcolm Lowry's "Volcano": Myth, Symbol, Meaning* (New York: Times Books, 1978), that the novel's many-layered symbolism, far from being ambiguous, is as carefully patterned as that of Joyce's later works and that what the *Volcano* demands is the sort of exegesis to which Stuart Gilbert subjected *Ulysses*. Markson provides the most detailed commentary on *Under the Volcano* that we have, but his study is unfortunately marred, on the one hand, by a hazy definition of its central concept—"by 'myth'. . . is meant *any* prototypal image" (p. 4)—and, on the other, by a misplaced concreteness: many of Lowry's allusions, which typically transpire in a halo of implication, are reduced to brittle equations. Even if one were persuaded that Lowry had in mind all the mythic and literary antecedents Markson adduces, the question remains whether many of them were not more important as a kind of scaffolding for the novelist, a means of stacking hoards of mental lumber, while he was constructing his book than they are likely to be to readers of the finished work. In any case, the master design in terms of which those motifs that are in fact crucial to the *Volcano* mesh does not emerge with much distinctness in Markson's study.

Tony Kilgallin's *Lowry* (Erin, Ontario: Press Porcepic, 1973) is concerned primarily with cataloging the literary and cinematic sources of many passages in *Ultramarine, Under the Volcano,* and the early stories. This background information throws considerable light on Lowry's symbolism, much of which is indeed esoteric, but it does not in itself make for a coherent view of the fiction. Kilgallin chooses not to deal with the later writings, although he does report, often verbatim, the recollections of people in British Columbia who knew Lowry while he was composing those works. Kilgallin's interviews constitute an important sup-

plement to Day's account of the Dollarton years. The most satis-
fying of the symbolist-oriented studies is Christine Pagnoulle's
Malcolm Lowry: Voyage au fond de nos abîmes (Lausanne: L'Age
d'Homme, 1977), which devotes two chapters to *Hear Us O Lord*
and the remainder to the *Volcano*. Although she does not discuss
the mimetic base of the novel at any length, she is acutely aware
of it and that consciousness enables her to analyze leitmotifs with
delicacy and restraint. Pagnoulle indicates the network these correspondences form without recourse to false systematizing, cabalistic or other.

Richard Hauer Costa's *Malcolm Lowry* (New York: Twayne,
1972) also succeeds in keeping the symbolic dimension of the fiction in perspective. His account of the kinship between Lowry and
his mentor Conrad Aiken is particularly valuable. The main
problem with Costa's book is that it confines itself to treating
aspects of the writer's life and work, and, sensible as many of
those discussions are, they give us no clear sense either of the
governing design of individual narratives or of the connections
among them. Muriel C. Bradbrook's *Malcolm Lowry: His Art
and Early Life* (London and New York: Cambridge Univ. Press,
1974) stresses the novelist's English roots. If the shores of Burrard Inlet symbolize paradise regained, she speculates, then his
childhood on the Wirral Peninsula represents the first Eden. As
one born in the same town as Lowry and as his contemporary at
Cambridge, she is able to fill in portions of the biography where
Day's material is relatively meager, and she argues persuasively
that the novelist's early history finds important echoes in his later
work. Bradbrook is more attentive to narrative values than most
critics, and she is more inclined than any of those mentioned
above to take the minor fiction seriously. Indeed she seems too
generous in her appraisal of much of it. *October Ferry* she treats
as though it were a triumph nearly equal to the *Volcano* rather
than being, as I see it, an instructive—albeit in its own way heroic
—failure.

Three brief introductions to the novelist's *oeuvre* warrant mention: Daniel B. Dodson's *Malcolm Lowry,* Columbia Essays on Modern Writers 51 (New York and London: Columbia Univ. Press, 1970), William H. New's *Malcolm Lowry,* Canadian Writers Series 11 (Toronto: McClelland and Stewart, 1971), and David Miller's *Malcolm Lowry and the Voyage that Never Ends* (London: Enitharmon Press, 1976). Of these Dodson's is the most sensible in its critical assessments, while New's offers a fuller account of the minor fiction than the other two. There are, in addition, three collections, the material in each of which varies considerably in merit. George Woodcock's *Malcolm Lowry: The Man and His Work* (Vancouver: Univ. of British Columbia Press, 1971) consists mainly of critical articles, source studies, and biographical reminiscenses, most of which had appeared earlier in *Canadian Literature.* In *Malcolm Lowry: Psalms and Songs* (New York and Scarborough, Ontario: New American Library, 1975), Margerie Lowry has gathered a number of fugitive pieces by and about her husband, including a series of intriguing memoirs (all but one of which had been previously published). Probably the most useful of these three volumes is Anne Smith's *The Art of Malcolm Lowry* (London: Vision Press, 1978), which contains eight new essays by different critics together with Russell Lowry's reflections on his brother.

Notes

ABBREVIATIONS
Apart from the first citation of a given story or novel in each
chapter, page references to the editions of Lowry's works listed
below are inserted directly in the text, preceded by the indicated
sigla:

D: *Dark as the Grave Wherein My Friend Is Laid.* Ed. Douglas
Day and Margerie Lowry. New York: New American Library,
1968.

F: *October Ferry to Gabriola.* Ed. Margerie Lowry. New York
and Cleveland: World, 1970.

H: *Hear Us O Lord from Heaven Thy Dwelling Place.* Philadelphia and New York: Lippincott, 1961.

P: *Malcolm Lowry: Psalms and Songs.* Ed. Margerie Lowry. New
York and Scarborough, Ontario: New American Library,
1975.

U: *Ultramarine.* Rev. ed. Philadelphia and New York: Lippincott, 1962.

V: *Under the Volcano.* Philadelphia and New York: Lippincott,
1965.

CHAPTER ONE
1. Arthur Calder-Marshall, quoted in Conrad Knickerbocker,
"Swinging the Paradise Street Blues: Malcolm Lowry in England," *Paris Review* 38 (summer 1966): 34.
2. *Finnegans Wake* (New York: Viking, 1958), p. 185.
3. *Ushant* (New York: Duell, Sloan, and Pearce; Boston:
Little Brown, 1952), p. 292.

4. To Albert Erskine, 22 June 1946, *The Selected Letters of Malcolm Lowry*, ed. Harvey Breit and Margerie Bonner Lowry (Philadelphia and New York: Lippincott, 1965), p. 113.

5. Lowry's having permitted an early draft of *Lunar Caustic* to be translated into French ("Le caustique lunaire," trans. Michèle d'Astorg and Clarisse Francillon, *L'Esprit* 24 [1956]: 111-14, 340-55, 525-43) shortly before his death indicates his eagerness to have the novella in print. "I am dying to see a copy of *Lunar Caustic* in your translation," he told Mlle Francillon. "Also I am longing to know how it went over in France" (*Letters,* p. 385). The fact that Lowry preferred to have the translators work from one of the early versions, rather than collating several drafts as the editors of the posthumous edition have done, suggests that the author might have been less than enthusiastic about the form in which his work was presented to British and American readers. Never convinced that any of his writings had attained finality, he once proposed to Robert Giroux that the latter publish *Lunar Caustic* in three versions, thus allowing the reader to witness the drama of a work "trying to integrate itself" (unpublished letter of 11 January 1952 in the University of British Columbia Lowry collection).

6. *Ultramarine* (1933; rev. ed. Philadelphia and New York: Lippincott, 1962), p. 143. On the matter of allusions in the novel to Eliot and others, see Ronald Binns, "Lowry's Anatomy of Melancholy," *Canadian Literature* 64 (spring 1975): 9-12.

7. As with many of the issues that divided father and son, these two disagreements ended in compromise. Malcolm went to sea for a year and subsequently took a B.A. in English at St. Catherine's College, Cambridge, submitting a draft of *Ultramarine* as his thesis. Upon his son's graduation, the elder Lowry offered him a position in the family firm and, when this was declined, a monthly stipend in its stead. None of these arrangements was very satisfactory. Malcolm foolishly allowed his father to get him a cabin boy's berth through business connections and then rode to the wharf in Arthur Lowry's chauffeur-driven limousine, both actions that his shipmates naturally resented. His university studies appear to have been largely a waste. After the freedom of the sea, the young man found the Cambridge curriculum stulti-

fying and was probably fortunate to get third class honors in the English tripos. One can scarcely judge whether the allowance was proffered out of generosity or a sense of obligation, but in either case it was hedged with humiliating conditions. Malcolm was at various times required to do such things as live in a temperance hotel and report all his movements to a solicitor appointed by his father. The novelist lived for the better part of two decades on the small sum he received each month, and one has only to read his correspondence to appreciate how much this form of dependence cost him emotionally. Reliable information about Lowry's early years is exceedingly difficult to obtain. Russell Lowry ("Malcolm —A Closer Look," *The Art of Malcolm Lowry,* ed. Anne Smith [London: Vision Press, 1978], pp. 9–27) has challenged all the published accounts of his younger brother's childhood and youth except that of M. C. Bradbrook in *Malcolm Lowry: His Art and Early Life* (London and New York: Cambridge Univ. Press, 1974). Perhaps the most revealing feature of Russell Lowry's memoir is its fundamental lack of sympathy for or understanding of the artist's work. He offers a substantially different—and, it may well be, more accurate—version of many events in his brother's history than had previously been current, but he does nothing, however much he tries, to dispel one's sense of how utterly a stranger Malcolm must have felt himself in his own family.

8. To Conrad Aiken, ca. 1932, *Letters,* p. 8.

9. To David Markson, 25 August 1951, *Letters,* p. 249. *Blue Voyage* was dedicated to C. M. L., the initials of Aiken's second wife, Clarissa Lorenz. Lowry's first name, which he dropped after leaving school, was Clarence.

10. On p. 52 of *Blue Voyage* (New York: Scribner's, 1927) the sea is actually referred to as "the ultramarine abyss." Lowry confessed to Aiken that *"Blue Voyage,* apart from its being the best nonsecular statement of the plight of the creative artist with the courage to live in the modern world, has become part of my consciousness & I cannot conceive of any other way in which *Ultramarine* might be written. . . . Nevertheless, I have sat & read my blasted book with increasing misery: with a misery of such intensity that I believe myself sometimes to be dispossessed, a spectre of your own discarded ideas" (unpublished letter, dating from

the early 1930s, in the U. B. C. Lowry collection). On the question of Aiken's influence on *Ultramarine,* see Douglas Day, *Malcolm Lowry* (New York: Oxford Univ. Press, 1973), pp. 102-8, 169-72, Richard H. Costa, *Malcolm Lowry* (New York: Twayne, 1972), pp. 37-40, and Geoffrey Durrant, "Aiken and Lowry," *Canadian Literature* 64 (spring 1975): 24-40.

11. *Ushant,* p. 355. *Ultramarine* and the other early works we shall be considering in this chapter do little to make Lowry's challenge to his master credible, but insofar as *Under the Volcano* accomplished what Aiken merely aimed at doing in his novels the prophecy has been fulfilled. One should of course add that Aiken's reputation depends more on his poetry than on his fiction.

12. *Letters,* p. 16. In a letter of 30 June 1946 concerning possible echoes in the *Volcano,* Lowry speaks of his "slight neurosis" on the subject of plagiarism, "due doubtless to an Elizabethan unscrupulousness in my evil youth in other works mercifully forgotten save by the author's medieval conscience" (*Letters,* p. 115). See Hallvard Dahlie, "Lowry's Debt to Grieg," *Canadian Literature* 64 (spring 1975): 41-51, for an analysis of resemblances between *Ultramarine* and *The Ship Sails On.*

13. *Under the Volcano* (1947; Philadelphia and New York: Lippincott, 1965), p. 21.

14. The notes for *In Ballast* are housed, together with a great mass of Lowry MSS, in the Special Collections Division of the U. B. C. Library.

15. *Ulysses* (New York: Modern Library, 1961), p. 208.

16. Sherrill Grace relates this "vision of the chaotic flux which Dana must accept" to the imagery of enclosing circles, symbols of the protagonist's self-encapsulation, present at many points in *Ultramarine* ("Outward Bound," *Canadian Literature* 67 [winter 1976]: 75).

17. *Letters,* p. 113.

18. Freud remarks of the oedipal project: "All [the child's] instincts, those of tenderness, gratitude, lustfulness, defiance and independence, find satisfaction in the single wish *to be his own father*" ("A Special Type of Choice of Object Made by Men," *The Standard Edition of the Complete Psychological*

Works of Sigmund Freud, trans. and ed. James Strachey et al. [London: Hogarth Press, 1953–74] 11:173).

19. *Letters,* p. 8. The date of the letter is circa 1932. In an extraordinary missive of 22 April 1942, Arthur Lowry rebukes his thirty-two-year-old son for his prodigal ways, in particular his disastrous marriage to Jan and his disregard for the feelings and desires of his parents. The letter, replete with biblical citations, is now in the U. B. C. Lowry collection, together with two drafts of the son's dutiful and contrite reply, which remains unpublished. That Malcolm wished to continue receiving the monthly allowance from his father may cast doubt on the sincerity of his penitence, but the stipend is itself proof of his prolonged dependence.

20. "Hotel Room in Chartres," *Story,* September 1934, reprinted in *Malcolm Lowry: Psalms and Songs,* ed. Margerie Lowry (New York and Scarborough, Ontario: New American Library, 1975), p. 22.

Psalms and Songs contains, besides "Hotel Room in Chartres," four other stories from the early and middle 1930s. "Seductio ad Absurdum" and "On Board the *West Hardaway,*" both early versions of incidents incorporated in *Ultramarine,* first appeared, respectively, in *Best British Short Stories of 1931,* ed. E. J. O'Brien (New York: Dodd, Mead, 1931), pp. 89–107, and *Story,* October 1933, pp. 12–22. "June the 30th, 1934" consists almost entirely of dialogue between a young clergyman prone to hysteria and an older man, a prospector for metals, as they journey from Paris to London. Weighing upon the two men is a sense that war, depression, and the decay of civilized values gravely threaten the life of Europe. The prospector is called Firmin, the first instance of that name in Lowry's fiction. The character in this story has little in common with the hero of *Under the Volcano,* however, apart from his having served in World War I and his suffering from lameness as a result of it. "China" belongs to the same body of experience from which the novelist drew *Ultramarine* and centers on its protagonist's contention that each of us lies imprisoned in his own consciousness: "the ground you tread on is your ground: it is never China or Siberia or England or anywhere else. ... It is always you. ... And you carry your horizon in your pocket wherever you are" (P54). A fifth story, "Enter One in

Sumptuous Armour," is grouped with those written during the period of Lowry's residence in Canada (1939–54), but its subject, derived from schoolboy encounters upon the playing fields of the Leys, Cambridge, and its lack of technical sophistication incline one to bracket it with the earlier pieces. None of the last three stories was published during the author's lifetime. What interest they have is biographical; they add nothing significant to our knowledge of Lowry's artistic development.

21. Norman O. Brown comments: "The *animal symbolicum* (Cassirer's definition of man) is *animal sublimans,* committed to substitute symbolical gratification of instincts for real gratification. . . . By the same token the *animal symbolicum* is the animal which has lost its world and life, and which preserves in its symbol systems a map of the lost reality, guiding the search to recover it" (*Life Against Death* [Middletown, Conn.: Wesleyan University Press, 1959], p. 167).

22. To David Markson, 25 August 1951, *Letters,* p. 261. In June 1937 Conrad Aiken addressed the following remarks to the psychoanalyst Henry Murray: "I'm reading Malcolm's really remarkable new novel, unpublished, very queer, very profound, very twisted, wonderfully rich—In Ballast to the White Sea. Gosh, the fellow's got genius—such a brilliant egocentric nonstop selfanalysis, and such a magnificent fountain, inexhaustible, of projected self-love I never did see. Wonderful. Too much of it, and directionless, but for sheer tactile richness and beauty of prose texture a joy to swim in" (*Selected Letters,* ed. Joseph Killorin [New Haven and London: Yale Univ. Press, 1978], p. 218).

23. "In Le Havre," *Life and Letters* 10 (1934): 464. In the sentence immediately following the Englishman's attack on his wife, he says: "You can have the custody of the child." This solitary reference to "the child" is a loose end in the story. Unless the child is the offspring of a previous marriage or has been conceived out of wedlock, its existence is hard to reconcile with the fact that the couple have been married only five months. It might be, of course, that Lee is pregnant; however, this seems unlikely, since she has just been in the hospital for what—if I read the husband's implications correctly—was surely an abortion. In his characteristic reflexive manner, he speaks as though the opera-

tion had been performed upon himself: "God, I feel dead: I feel as though my whole inside had been taken out: all I feel inside is a smouldering hollow" (p. 462).

24. Lowry habitually referred to his father in his conversations and letters as "the old man." A good many of his actions may, it seems, be explained in terms of their antagonism. One of the novelist's friends from his London period, James Hepburn, recalls: "The fact that Malcolm could drink sixteen pints of beer and a half-bottle of whiskey somehow evened things up between him and the old man" (quoted in Knickerbocker, p. 33). It seems plausible that the author was concerned with "getting one back" not just on Arthur Lowry but on Aiken as well. Given the younger writer's perception of his mentor's ambivalent motives for introducing him to Jan Gabrial, it is quite possible that Lowry's marital failure was meant to punish his substitute father as much as his actual one.

25. "In Le Havre," p. 463.

26. *Lunar Caustic*, ed. Earle Birney and Margerie Lowry, *Paris Review*, no. 29 (winter–spring 1963), reprinted in *Psalms and Songs*, p. 266.

27. To James Stern, 7 May 1940, *Letters*, p. 28.

28. To Derek Pethick, 6 March 1950, *Letters*, p. 197. Lowry claimed that his maternal grandfather, Captain Lyon Boden, ordered a British gunboat to sink his windjammer, *The Scottish Isles*, whose crew was dying of cholera. Tony Kilgallin repeats this account with a significant variation: Lyon Boden "died at twenty-eight of cholera in the Indian Ocean and, in what would come to be called a 'typically Lowryesque' correspondence, the ship that he had captained was lost shortly thereafter in a storm" (*Lowry* [Erin, Ont.: Press Porcepic, 1973], p. 13). Douglas Day, on the other hand, reports: "It is true that there once was an outbreak of cholera aboard *The Scottish Isles;* but it is also true that Captain Boden died peacefully in his bed, at the age of 90, in 1934" (*Malcolm Lowry*, p. 59). Muriel C. Bradbrook's version of this incident parallels Kilgallin's in most details; she believes that Day has confused the date of Boden's death with that of his wife, who did indeed live to be ninety (*Malcolm Lowry*, pp. 25, 153). Whatever the facts about Lowry's grandfather may be, it is evi-

dent that the artist's anecdote concerning the captain was a characteristic instance of his personal myth making.

29. *Letters,* p. 197. Pethick was to offer an interpretation of the *Volcano* over the CBC radio network in which, Lowry declared with characteristic wryness, "the Consul is really Moby Dick masquerading as the unconsious aspect of the Cadbosaurus in the Book of Jonah, or words to that effect" (*Letters,* p. 196). Hence the author's reply is often tongue in cheek, but least so, it seems, in his observations on failure.

30. See Henry Murray's classic psychoanalytical essay on Melville, "In Nomine Diaboli," *New England Quarterly* 24 (1951): 435–52.

31. To Conrad Aiken, spring 1940, *Letters,* pp. 24–25.

32. *Moby-Dick,* ed. Harrison Hayford and Hershel Parker (New York: Norton, 1967), p. 358.

33. "Dithering crack" was one of the many phrases Lowry borrowed from Conrad Aiken. One suspects that Aiken's longstanding interest in Freud may have affected Lowry's attitude toward psychiatry almost as much as the latter's brief stay in Bellevue in June 1935 (see Day, pp. 196–97).

34. "Plantagenet," the family appellation of kings, seems closely akin to "Lawhill"; both obliquely indicate the fact that one does not, as a rule, choose one's own name, that one's public identity is thrust upon one by a superior force. Paradoxically, "Plantagenet," which means literally "sprig of broom," also calls attention to the capacity of natural beings to regenerate themselves, an undercurrent of hope that runs through *Lunar Caustic.* At a wharf beside the hospital lies a ruined coal barge, its hold choked with silt "through which emerald shoots had sprouted" (P261). "Plantagenet" is the first instance in Lowry's fiction of the author's penchant for bestowing broadly symbolic names on his characters.

35. For a catalog of jazz elements in *Lunar Caustic,* see Perle Epstein's essay "Swinging the Maelstrom" in *Malcolm Lowry: The Man and His Work,* ed. George Woodcock (Vancouver: Univ. of British Columbia Press, 1971), pp. 149–50.

36. In connection with Plantagenet's egocentricity, see Beverly Rasporich, "The Right Side of Despair: Lowry's Comic Spirit in

Lunar Caustic and *Dark as the Grave Wherein My Friend Is Laid,"* *Mosaic* 10 (summer 1977): 56–61.

37. In developing the relationship between the protagonist and the doctor, the posthumous edition of *Lunar Caustic* follows the account given in *The Last Address* (1936) more closely than it does the one in *Swinging the Maelstrom* (1940). In the latter version the psychiatrist, called Philip, is much more sensitive to the inmates' suffering than Claggart. Bill finds himself entering into a tacit collaboration with Philip, who happens to be his cousin, and thus becomes implicated in the continued suffering of Kalowsky and Garry. For a perceptive discussion of the differing treatment of the doctor in the 1936 and 1940 versions of the novella, see David Benham, "Lowry's Purgatory," in *Malcolm Lowry: The Man and His Work,* pp. 59–60, 62–63.

38. Lowry remarks in an unpublished letter of 27 May 1956 to Clarisse Francillon that the version of *Lunar Caustic* she had translated "would be improved by another long chapter that provided more of a motivation for Plantagenet than he has" (U. B. C. Lowry collection).

39. *Civilization and Its Discontents, Standard Edition* 21:133.

40. In *Swinging the Maelstrom* the possibility of salvation, of acting to change oneself and society, remains open. At the end of this version of the novella Bill joins a ship bringing aid to the Spanish Loyalists, just as Hugh Firmin intends to do in the *Volcano.* Cf. Benham, p. 63.

41. To Albert Erskine, March 1952, *Letters,* p. 292.

42. *Le Voyage, Oeuvres complètes,* ed. Y.-G. LeDantec and Claude Pichois (Paris: Pléiade, 1961), p. 123.

43. There is some question about the exact date of the Lowrys' arrival in Mexico. Day argues that it probably occurred on either November 1 or 2, the latter being *el Día de los Difuntos* (*Malcolm Lowry,* p. 214).

44. To John Davenport, December 1937, *Letters,* pp. 12–13.

CHAPTER TWO

1. *Under the Volcano* (1947; Philadelphia and New York: Lippincott, 1965), p. 355.

2. To Jonathan Cape, 2 January 1946, *Selected Letters of Mal-*

colm Lowry, ed. Harvey Breit and Margerie Bonner Lowry (Philadelphia and New York: Lippincott, 1965), p. 59. Virtually all those who have written on Lowry since 1965 have recognized the thirty-page letter to his publisher as a seminal point for the exegesis of the *Volcano.* Unless otherwise indicated, all references to the novelist's correspondence in this chapter are to the Cape letter.

3. See, for example, Terence Wright, *"Under the Volcano:* The Static Art of Malcolm Lowry," *Ariel* 1 (1970): 67–76, Victor Doyen, "Elements towards a Spatial Reading of Malcolm Lowry's *Under the Volcano," English Studies* 50 (1969): 65–74, Sherrill E. Grace, *"Under the Volcano:* Narrative Mode and Technique," *Journal of Canadian Fiction* 2 (spring 1973): 57–61, and Jonathan Arac, "The Form of Carnival in *Under the Volcano," PMLA* 92 (1977): 487–88.

4. *Letters,* p. 67.

5. See the letter to Derek Pethick, 6 March 1950, *Letters,* p. 198.

6. *Letters,* p. 58. The fullest discussion of Mexico as a setting for the novel occurs in Ronald G. Walker, *Infernal Paradise: Mexico and the Modern English Novel* (Berkeley and Los Angeles: Univ. of California Press, 1978), pp. 237–80.

7. Presenting *Under the Volcano* to French readers, Lowry declared that the book "has for its subject the forces that dwell within man and lead him to look upon himself with terror ("Preface to a Novel," trans. George Woodcock, *Malcolm Lowry: The Man and His Work,* ed. Woodcock [Vancouver: Univ. of British Columbia Press, 1971], p. 14). See Stephen Tifft, "Tragedy as a Meditation on Itself: Reflexiveness in *Under the Volcano," The Art of Malcolm Lowry,* ed. Anne Smith (London: Vision Press, 1978), pp. 46–71.

8. *Letters,* p. 67.

9. *The Savage God* (New York: Random House, 1971), p. 147.

10. The most penetrating analysis of the style is Brian O'Kill's "Aspects of Language in *Under the Volcano," The Art of Malcolm Lowry,* pp. 72–92.

11. See Albert J. Guerard's remarks on the Consul's sexuality, and in particular his latent homoeroticism, in "The Illuminating

Distortion," *Novel* 5 (1972): 116–17.

12. *Finnegans Wake* (New York: Viking, 1958), p. 489.

13. On Marlowe's and Goethe's dramas as sources for the novel, see Anthony R. Kilgallin, "Faust and *Under the Volcano*," *Malcolm Lowry: The Man and His Work*, pp. 26–37, and Stefan Makowiecki, "Symbolic Pattern in *Under the Volcano*," *Kwartalnik Neofilologiczny* 23 (1976): 455–63.

14. *Letters*, p. 71. On the wheel imagery and the theme of recurrence, see Kristofer Dorosz, *Malcolm Lowry's Infernal Paradise* (Uppsala: Acta Universitatis Upsaliensis, 1976), pp. 147–50, and Christine Pagnoulle, *Malcolm Lowry: Voyage au fond de nos abîmes* (Lausanne: L'Age d'Homme, 1977), pp. 49, 93–94, 107, 125.

15. On the significance that the sea has for each of the principal characters, see Bernadette Wild, "Malcolm Lowry: A Study of the Sea Metaphor in *Under the Volcano*," *University of Windsor Review* 4 (fall 1968): 46–60.

16. Chapter 2 is narrated from Yvonne's point of view, but Lowry does not adhere to it slavishly. When it suits his purpose, he subtly shifts from Yvonne to Geoffrey and back again, a tactic for which the contrapuntal dialogue emanating from the other side of the partition has prepared the reader. Even if one assumes, though, that Yvonne does imagine what is going through the Consul's mind, it is difficult to suppose that she has much sympathetic understanding of these contents.

17. *The Divided Self* (Harmondsworth: Penguin, 1965), p. 112. "The need to be perceived is not, of course, purely a visual affair,' comments Laing. "It extends to the general need to have one's presence endorsed or confirmed by the other, the need for one's total existence to be recognized; the need, in fact, to be loved" (p. 119).

No more poignant statement of this craving exists than the following one in Ford Madox Ford's *The Good Soldier* (New York: Knopf, 1951), p. 115: "We are all so afraid, we are all so alone, we all so need from the outside the assurance of our own worthiness to exist." There is a marked affinity between Ford's novel and *Under the Volcano.* Both probe divisions within the self, lay bare the contradictions of the heart, by playing on the erotic variations that unfold among a quartet of characters. Cf. "A Prose Waste Land," *TLS* 61 (1962): 338.

18. *Moby-Dick,* ed. Harrison Hayford and Hershel Parker (New York: Norton, 1967), p. 147. See my essay *"Moby-Dick* and *Under the Volcano:* Poetry from the Abyss," *Modern Fiction Studies* 20 (1974): 149–56, and Jean-Roger Carroy, "De Melville à Lowry, et retour par nos abîmes," *Les lettres nouvelles* 2–3 (May–June 1974): 123–69.

19. "Popo was quite clear earlier, remember? Now he looks like a whale...Moby Dick," Hugh said, "that is, both a whale and a God" (B MS, chap. 4, p. 28, in the University of British Columbia Lowry collection). The first extant version of the full novel in the U. B. C. archives is designated the B MS. The D MS referred to in subsequent notes is a later draft of this version, the one submitted to American publishers in 1940–41. On the evolution of the book, see Douglas Day, *Malcolm Lowry* (New York: Oxford Univ. Press. 1973), pp. 258–74, Richard Hauer Costa, *Malcolm Lowry* (New York: Twayne, 1972), pp. 88–103, and Victor Doyen, "La genèse d'"Au-dessous du Volcan,'" *Les lettres nouvelles* 2–3 (May–June 1974): 87–122.

20. *Moby-Dick,* p. 443.

21. In his letter to Cape, Lowry speaks of the arcane elements in *Under the Volcano* in a way that recalls Yeats's metaphorical disposition of the material in *A Vision:* "The Cabbala is used for poetical purposes because it represents man's spiritual aspiration. The Tree of Life, which is its emblem, is a kind of complicated ladder with Kether, or Light, at the top and an extremely unpleasant abyss some way above the middle. The Consul's spiritual domain in this regard is probably the Qliphoth, the world of shells and demons, represented by the Tree of Life upside down." One commentator, Perle Epstein (*The Private Labyrinth of Malcolm Lowry* [New York: Holt, Rinehart, and Winston, 1969]), constructs an ingenious allegorical reading of the *Volcano* based on these doctrines. The author's initiation into cabalistic lore came, however, relatively late in his composition of the novel, and he himself indicates, in the lines that follow the preceding quotation, that it is "not important at all to the understanding of the book; I just mention it in passing to hint that, as Henry James

says, 'There are depths'" (*Letters*, p. 65).

22. The classic description of psychical impotence is Freud's paper "On the Universal Tendency to Debasement in the Sphere of Love," *The Standard Edition of the Complete Psychological Works of Sigmund Freud,* trans. and ed. James Strachey et al. (London: Hogarth Press, 1953–74) 11:177–90. See David Markson, *Malcolm Lowry's "Volcano": Myth, Symbol, Meaning* (New York: Times Books, 1978), p. 52, for a different psychological explanation.

23. "In the Cabbala, the misuse of magical powers is compared to drunkenness," remarks the novelist. "William James if not Freud would certainly agree with me when I say that the agonies of the drunkard find their most accurate poetic analogue in the agonies of the mystic who has abused his powers" (*Letters,* p. 71). See James, *The Varieties of Religious Experience* (New York: Longmans, Green, 1903), pp. 386–87.

24. "Vergönne mir, ihn zu belehren," pleads Gretchen at the close of *Faust,* pt. 2; "noch blendet ihn der neue Tag" (lines 12092–93). Yvonne's radiance represents, on the cabalistic plane, the Shekinah or female emanation of the godhead, and it suggests also the "woman clothed with the sun" in Revelation 12:1, an apparition of the Mater Gloriosa.

25. The hope of renewal is not altogether visionary, at least not in the pejorative sense of the word. Lowry himself pulled back from the precipice and went in 1940 with his second wife Margerie to live on the beach at Dollarton, B.C. There he achieved the Apollonian/Dionysian balance of soul and body that enabled him, no *Übermensch,* to complete *Under the Volcano.* Eridanus is, as one might suspect, modeled closely upon Dollarton. In the same year that the Lowrys moved to their shack on Burrard Inlet, thirteen American publishers rejected an early version of the *Volcano.* What seemed at the time a lethal blow turned out to be a fortunate development, for in the years between 1940 and 1944 Lowry undertook the revisions that gave the novel its quality of tragic affirmation. Nothing comparable to the Eridanus theme, the essential counterpoint of hope, exists in the earlier drafts.

26. *Letters,* p. 74.

27. Cf. *Ushant* (New York: Duell, Sloan, and Pearce; Boston:

Little, Brown, 1952), p. 357. For a cogent discussion of the way Joycean techniques were transmitted to Lowry via *Blue Voyage,* see Richard Costa, *Malcolm Lowry,* pp. 28–44.

28. Douglas Day comments perceptively on the humor, wry and compassionate, of the *Volcano* in "Of Tragic Joy," *Prairie Schooner* 37 (1963–64): 354–62.

29. *Letters,* p. 77.

30. See Freud's analysis of compulsive repetition in *Beyond the Pleasure Principle,* particularly his remarks on the case of a "good little boy" (*Standard Edition,* 18:14–17).

31. Sylvia Plath's poems offer striking examples of a comparable suicidal drive to rejoin a dead parent, much loved and resented, and to dissolve the barriers between self and other. Consider these lines from "Daddy":

> I tried to die
> And get back, back, back to you.
> I thought even the bones would do.

Or those in "Ariel" where the poet describes the impulse to merge her "I" with the sun, "the red / Eye, the cauldron of morning" (*Ariel* [New York: Harper, 1965], pp. 51, 27).

32. Lowry appropriated the figure of the bookish seventeenth-century recluse Blackstone (not to be confused with the jurist) from Aiken, who had become interested in him as early as 1925 and who was ultimately to use him as a prototype for his hero in *The Kid* (New York: Duell, Sloan, and Pearce, 1947).

33. William H. Gass makes this passage the focal point of a stunning essay, "In Terms of the Toenail: Fiction and the Figures of Life." His thesis is that "the novel does not say, it shows; it shows me my life in a figure: it compels me to stare at my toes. . . . The novelist makes a system for us . . . composed of a host of particulars, arranged to comply with esthetic conditions, and it both flatters and dismays us when we look at our life through it because our life appears holy and beautiful always, even when tragic and ruthlessly fated" (*Fiction and the Figures of Life* [New York: Knopf, 1970], p. 71). For a telling critique of the anti-mimetic, idealizing position espoused by Gass, see Charles Bax-

ter, "The Escape from Irony: *Under the Volcano* and the Aesthetics of Arson," *Novel* 10 (1977): 114–26.

34. The passage occurs in chapter 12 of the 1940 version (D MS, p. 341, U. B. C. Lowry collection).

35. In a letter of 1 March 1950 to Clarisse Francillon, Lowry wrote: "I wondered if you could somehow smuggle a copy, with my compliments, of your translation [of the *Volcano*] to Jean Cocteau, and tell him I have never forgotten his kindness in giving me a seat for *La Machine infernale* at the Champs Elysées in May, 1934: I went to see it on 2 successive days and I shall never forget the marvellous performance as long as I live. . . . And so you see his infernal machine comes back to torment the Consul in Chapter VII" (*Letters*, p. 192). In his "Preface to a Novel," the author remarks that the *Volcano* itself "can be thought of as a kind of machine; it works, you may be sure, for I have discovered that to my own expense" (p. 14).

36. See Dale Edmonds, *"Under the Volcano:* A Reading of the 'Immediate Level,'" *Tulane Studies in English* 16 (1968): 77–79, for a concise account of the pertinent aspects of Mexican politics in the middle and late 1930s.

37. Lowry identified the Indian's plight with that of "mankind himself, mankind dying—then, in the Battle of the Ebro, or now, in Europe, while we do nothing, or if we would, have put ourselves in a position where we *can* do nothing, but talk, while he goes on dying. . . . The incident by the roadside, based on a personal experience, was the germ of the book" (*Letters*, p. 79). A short story entitled "Under the Volcano," purportedly the original version of chapter 8, appeared in *Prairie Schooner* 37 (1963–64): 284–300. Brian O'Kill argues, in a letter to the editor of *TLS* (73 [1974]: 447), that the published story is not the initial piece Lowry wrote in 1936 but rather that excerpt from an intermediate draft of the *Volcano* to which the author refers in a letter to Harold Matson of 4 March 1941 (*Letters,* p. 39).

38. The author insisted that the *Volcano* was, among other things, a "horse opera" (*Letters*, p. 66). Geoffrey's heroics seem to anticipate the histrionic last stand of Clare Quilty in *Lolita,* although the impact of the two scenes is quite different. Nabokov

burlesques the traditional death scene, while Lowry heightens the intensity of a fundamentally tragic development by rubbing against the grain.

39. The question of who is to blame for what occurs in Parián is sensitively explored in Andrew J. Pottinger, "The Consul's 'Murder,'" *Canadian Literature* 67 (winter 1976): 53–63.

40. The Consul's words to the dog echo ones spoken by Nordahl Grieg's protagonist in *The Ship Sails On,* trans. A. G. Chater (New York: Knopf, 1927). As Benjamin is on the verge of leaping into the sea with the ship's dog in his arms, he declaims: "Santos, . . . this day shalt thou be with me in paradise" (p. 217; cf. Luke 23:43). Lowry manages to put a sharp ironic point on an incident that is, in Grieg's novel, impossibly melodramatic.

41. On Yvonne as an Electra figure, see Markson, p. 131.

42. "I intended . . . the feeling of hope per se to transcend even one's interest in the characters." declared the author (*Letters,* p. 80).

43. *Oeuvres complètes de Baudelaire,* ed. Y.-G. LeDantec and Claude Pichois (Paris: Pléiade, 1961), p. 44. "Why do people see rats?" asks the Consul. "Consider the word remorse. Remord. Mordeo, mordere. La Mordida! Agenbite too. . . And why rongeur? Why all this biting, all those rodents, in the etymology? (V218–19)

44. *Oeuvres complètes,* p. 42.

45. *Letters,* p. 81.

46. "Kubla Khan," *The Complete Poetical Works of Samuel Taylor Coleridge,* ed. E. H. Coleridge (Oxford: Clarendon, 1912) 1:297.

47. "Dreams of missing a train," explains Freud, "are dreams of consolation for [one] kind of anxiety felt in sleep—the fear of dying. 'Departing' on a journey is one of the commonest and best authenticated symbols of death. These dreams say in a consoling way: 'Don't worry, you won't die (depart)'. . . . The difficulty of understanding [such] dreams is due to the fact that the feeling of anxiety is attached precisely to the expression of consolation" (*The Interpretation of Dreams, Standard Edition* 5:385). That Lowry was aware of the bearing this theory had on the opening of chapter 10 is evident from his statement that the "train theme is

related to Freudian death dreams" (*Letters,* p. 81).

48. "En es-tu donc venue à ce point d'engourdissement que tu ne te plaises que dans ton mal?" the poet asks his soul. "S'il en est ainsi, fuyons vers le pays qui sont les analogies de la Mort." Mexico is, for the Consul, just such a deathscape. At the end of Baudelaire's poem the soul responds: "N'importe où! n'importe où! pourvu que ce soit hors de ce monde!" ("Any Where Out of the World," *Oeuvres complètes,* p. 304).

49. In a letter to Derek Pethick of 6 March 1950, Lowry comments that his protagonist "has almost ceased to be a man altogether, and his human feelings merely make matters more agonizing for him, but don't alter things in the least; he is thus in hell" (*Letters,* p. 200).

50. See Robert Graves, *The Greek Myths* (Baltimore: Penguin, 1955) 1:151–53. A similar occurrence takes place in the penultimate chapter of *Ulysses,* in which a star is precipitated from Lyra to Leo. Bloom, the Leo in question, and Stephen, the all-too-lyric artist, become in *Ithaca* "heavenly bodies, wanderers like the stars at which they gaze. The last word...is left to Penelope. This is the indispensable countersign to Bloom's passport to eternity" (*Letters of James Joyce,* ed. Stuart Gilbert [New York: Viking, 1957] 1:160).

51. *Letters,* p. 83.

52. *Letters,* p. 84. See Pagnoulle, pp. 121–25, for a perceptive treatment of the way in which chapter 11 oscillates between the stellar and mundane levels of meaning.

53. See *Letters,* pp. 61, 85.

54. The María incident, upon which so much depends in the final version of the *Volcano,* was confined to a single paragraph in the 1940 draft. In the earlier version the Consul makes an ironic connection between his assignation with the prostitute and the phrase Faust employs to designate the moment in which his striving would cease: "As with a shamed grimace, he gave María ...her few pesos, a knowledge of what hell really was blazed on his soul. 'Verweile doch, du bist so schön,' he said, and laughed self-accusingly" (D MS, p. 382). Facing the passage just quoted, Lowry wrote in the margin: "This could be better dramatized."

In all drafts of the novel through 1940, Yvonne is cast as the

Consul's daughter, and at one point in the published version Geoffrey does in fact regard her in that light: "he'd half hoped all along Yvonne would come to rescue him, . . . if only as a daughter, who would understand and comfort him" (V360). Were she his child rather than his wife, he would of course be relieved of the obligation to strike a balance between tenderness and sensuality in his relations with her.

55. For a discussion of other similarities between the two novels, see Robert B. Heilman, "The Possessed Artist and the Ailing Soul," *Malcolm Lowry: The Man and His work,* pp. 18–20. Of Mann's *Faustus,* which appeared in the same year as the *Volcano,* Lowry himself remarked: "His protagonist and mine seem to have raced almost neck and neck to perdition" (unpublished letter to Arabel Porter, 29 May 1953, U. B. C. Lowry collection).

56. In chapter 7 Geoffrey recalls a crippled beggar who "after four drinks from the Consul had taken him for the Christ, and falling down on his knees before him, had pinned swiftly under his coat-lapel two medallions, joined to a tiny worked bleeding heart like a pincushion, portraying the Virgin of Guadalupe" (V200). There are obvious similarities between Geoffrey and the alcoholic priest in *The Power and the Glory,* whose vocation seems, through much of the book, more a caricature than an imitation of Christ. In both cases the protagonists' drinking reflects a frustrated longing for religious communion. Greene's novel is, however, traditional in form, and its ultimate thrust is markedly different from that of the *Volcano. The Power and the Glory* expresses a piety that is, at bottom, orthodox and nowhere more so than in its rendering of the priest's martyrdom.

57. The scene outside the Farolito, with its atmosphere of unreality perforated by flashes of an all too actual horror, recalls the closing pages of *The Trial.* In both instances the guilt-ridden protagonists appear to collaborate with their executioners and, at the same time, to yearn for signs of compassion. The moments of solace Geoffrey experiences when an old fiddler calls him "compañero" or when he imagines various rescuers arriving find a counterpart in Joseph K.'s vision of a presence in the window of

an adjoining house: "a human figure, faint and insubstantial at that distance and that height, leaned abruptly far forward and stretched both arms still farther. Who was it? A friend? A good man? Someone who sympathized? Someone who wanted to help? Was it one person only? Or was it mankind?" (*The Trial*, trans. Willa and Edwin Muir [New York: Modern Library, n. d.], p. 286). In each case, those who inflict death do so in a manner calculated to degrade the victim: K. perishes, as he says, "like a dog"; the Consul's slayers throw a dead cur after his body into the barranca.

58. The 1940 version of the novel has as one of its epigraphs a quotation from Henry James, written within a day of Britain's entry into the First World War: "The plunge of civilization into this abyss of blood and darkness...is a thing that so gives away the whole long age during which we have supposed the world to be, with whatever abatement, gradually bettering, that to have to take it all now for what the treacherous years were all the while really making for and *meaning* is too tragic for any words" (*The Letters of Henry James*, ed. Percy Lubbock [New York: Scribner's, 1920] 2:384).

CHAPTER THREE

1. Unpublished letter to Harold Matson, 4 October 1940, in the University of British Columbia Lowry collection.

2. *Hear Us O Lord from Heaven Thy Dwelling Place* (Philadelphia and New York: Lippincott, 1961), p. 38.

3. Aside from the French translation of an early version of *Lunar Caustic* (see chap. 1, n. 5), Lowry published only two short stories from this body of work before his death, "Strange Comfort Afforded by the Profession," *New World Writing* 3 (1953): 331-44, and "The Bravest Boat," *Partisan Review*, 21 (1954): 275-88, both of which have been reprinted in *Hear Us O Lord*.

4. To Matson, 2 October 1951, in *Selected Letters of Malcolm Lowry*, ed. Harvey Breit and Margerie Bonner Lowry (Philadelphia and New York: Lippincott, 1965), p. 267.

5. To Albert Erskine, 29 October 1947, *Letters*, p. 157.

6. An examination of the manuscript in the U. B. C. Lowry

collection reveals that chapter 1 of *Dark as the Grave Wherein My Friend Is Laid* (New York: New American Library, 1968) is constituted as follows:

pp. 1–2, "The sense of speed...permanent panic": the opening paragraph of the second draft (MS, p. 383);

pp. 2–3, "Leaving Oregon...promise for the future": the beginning of the first draft (MS, pp. 1–2);

p. 3, "It was as if...a wild apple tree in bloom": MS, pp. 389–90, with a brief paragraph deleted;

pp. 3–12, "It had been a day...in the other's place": MS, pp. 2–14, with the following changes: dialogue elided on pp. 6–8, the name "Sam" changed to "Mauger" on p. 7, a passage italicized on pp. 7–8, and many cuts on p. 11;

p. 12, almost two pages of MS deleted;

pp. 12–17, "He could not help...another unit of two verses": MS, pp. 16–24, with fifteen lines of verse and some discursive matter omitted on p. 16 and additional cuts on p. 17;

p. 17, "How did it go?": supplied by the editors; the entirety of MS pp. 25–26 deleted;

p. 17, "Primrose was shaking him...The El Paso flight was on": MS, p. 27; no chapter division indicated in the MS.

7. George Woodcock, for example, regrets the editors' attempt "to present a relatively smooth running novel that would interest the intelligent general reader. They might have saved themselves the effort, for *Dark as the Grave*—one realizes in the first twenty pages—is likely to be of interest only to Lowry cultists and to literary scholars, and both groups would undoubtedly have preferred the novel in that unsmoothed chaos which would have told us so much more about the writer's mind and his ways of working" (*Odysseus Ever Returning* [Toronto and Montreal: McClelland and Stewart, 1970], p. 72). Matthew Corrigan decries "the idea that a man's unfinished work is not respectable unless it can somehow be stuffed into the mould of the novel, and advertised accordingly." He argues cogently that "when an author dies something happens to his work. It may become more important for his future reputation that the unfinished work remain so, rather than be brought to some kind of tentative and artificial conclusion" ("Malcolm Lowry, New York Publishing, and the

'New Illiteracy,'" *Encounter* 35 [July 1970], 83, 82). (Corrigan has, one should add, seen both sides of the issue. See his reviews of *Dark as the Grave* in the *Dalhousie Review* 48 [1968]: 419-21, and *Shenandoah* 19 [summer 1968]: 89-93; in the latter he claims that "the editors have done a remarkable job and almost every Lowry admirer will be grateful to them" [p. 89].) Douglas Day himself appears to have had misgivings about the editing of *Dark as the Grave*—at any rate, about the alterations that Margerie Lowry was making in the manuscript—even while the project was underway (see his *Malcolm Lowry* [New York: Oxford Univ. Press, 1973], p. 438n).

8. The name "Sigbjørn" translates from the Norwegian as "triumphant bear," *Sig-* being a combining form of the word for "victory" and *-bjørn* the Northern Germanic word for "bear." Norman J. Fry of the University of Florida reports that "Old Norse *bjarn* (usually in *bjarndýr*—'bear,' literally 'brown animal') is a form of the common Germanic root meaning 'brown,' and has been used in all Germanic dialects as a euphemism for totemic appeasement in place of the original Indo-European word for 'bear' seen in Latin *ursus* and Greek *árktos*." There is no telling whether Lowry was aware of this totemic overtone, but it accords, in any case, with the allegorical significance of the name.

9. Lowry, in his notes for *Dark as the Grave* (MS, p. 555), observes that his protagonist's life is "full of mysterious and terrifying events, from which he could deduce, if anyone could, the existence of the supernatural, of God: his tale should be considered as a kind of quest. . . less of a meaning in his life [than] of sufficient greatness of soul to accept unflinchingly the existence of a meaning and the knowledge that he will never know precisely what it is."

R. D. Laing provides a helpful gloss on the character of such "mysterious and terrifying events": "If the individual cannot take the realness, aliveness, autonomy, and identity of himself and others for granted, then he has to become absorbed in contriving ways of trying to be real, of keeping himself or others alive, of preserving his identity, in efforts, as he will often put it, to prevent himself losing his self. What are to most people everyday happenings, which are hardly noticed because they have no special significance, may become deeply significant in so far as they either contribute to the sustenance of the individual's being or threaten him with non-being" (*The Divided Self* [Harmondsworth: Penguin, 1965], pp. 42–43).

10. *Under the Volcano* (1947; Philadelphia and New York: Lippincott, 1965), p. 371.

Regarding the source of this material, Lowry relates, in a letter to James Stern of 7 May 1940: "I was thrown, for a time, in Mexico, as a spy, into durance vile, by some fascistas in Oaxaca (by mistake; they were after another man. How it arose was: he was a friend of mine, very sober and a communist, and they could not believe, because he was sober, that he was an agitator and therefore thought he must be me.)" (*Letters,* p. 29). Unfortunately nothing more is known about the writer's relationship with this person, called Hölscher in *Dark as the Grave,* who left his mark on chapter 12 of the *Volcano* (see Day, *Malcolm Lowry,* pp. 236–37).

11. Jan Gabrial offers another perspective on her parting from the artist in "Not with a Bang," *Story* 39 (September-October 1946): 53–61. One is astonished to discover how closely the experience recounted in her story and even the idiom in which the dialogue and thoughts of the husband and wife are cast mesh with *Under the Volcano.* According to Day, Lowry regarded "Not with a Bang" as "a cruelly accurate record of his final breakup with Jan" (*Malcolm Lowry,* p. 231).

12. Letter of 2 January 1946, *Letters,* p. 60.

13. The chapter on alcohol addiction in Karl Menninger's *Man against Himself* (New York: Harcourt, Brace, n. d.), pp. 140–61, throws much light on the predicament faced by Lowry and his protagonists.

14. In his working notes, Lowry distinguishes Primrose from women who are "fertile with broad hips." He means her to embody "something fragile and slender, another life principle far more subtle, far more spiritual than the cow" (U. B. C. Lowry collection).

15. *La Mordida,* as Lowry left it, resembles a notebook more nearly than it does a novel. Since the narrative is essentially a

continuation of the adventures related in *Dark as the Grave* and reflects the same preoccupations evident in that book, publication of it would be supererogatory. Its story line parallels the account of the Lowrys' difficulties with the Mexican immigration authorities given in a deposition of 15 June 1946 that the novelist filed with A. Ronald Button, a Los Angeles attorney (*Letters,* pp. 91–112). *La Mordida* contains several passages that treat the artist's problems with characterization, including the following one: "With very few exceptions the novelist who is anxious to show how much he loves his characters loves only himself, just in fact like dear old Sigbjørn. . . . The narcissism is indeed necessary —but the great characters. . . in Shakespeare, Romains, Tolstoy . . . seem to come about by a gigantic projection, or in the case of peopled novels a breaking down of the central atom of the author's. . . personality" (MS, p. 108).

16. To Cape, 2 January 1946, *Letters,* p. 60.

17. To Erskine, 29 October 1947, *Letters,* p. 157.

18. To Cape, 2 January 1946, *Letters,* p. 66. See Jonathan Arac's discussion of the book as a Menippean satire in "The Form of Carnival in *Under the Volcano,*" *PMLA* 92 (1977): 481–89.

19. See the observations by Earle Birney on his friend's drinking quoted in Tony Kilgallin, *Lowry* (Erin, Ont.: Press Porcepic, 1973), pp. 74–75.

20. To Erskine, early summer 1953, *Letters,* pp. 339–40.

21. Unpublished letter to Erskine, December 1953 (U. B. C. Lowry collection). On the problems Lowry encountered in his search for a new form, see Matthew Corrigan's essays, "The Writer as Consciousness: A View of *October Ferry to Gabriola,*" *Malcolm Lowry: The Man and His Work,* ed. George Woodcock (Vancouver: Univ. of British Columbia Press, 1971), pp. 71–77, and "Malcolm Lowry: The Phenomenology of Failure," *Boundary 2* 3 (1975): 407–42, and Barry Wood, "Malcolm Lowry's Metafiction: The Biography of a Genre," *Contemporary Literature* 19 (1978): 1–25.

22. See *Anatomy of Criticism* (Princeton Univ. Press, 1957), pp. 304–8.

23. To Erskine, early summer 1953, *Letters,* p. 339.

24. Introduction to Hugo von Hofmannsthal, *Selected Prose,* trans. Mary Hottinger and Tania and James Stern, Bollingen Series 33 (New York: Pantheon, 1952), pp. xviii–xix. Lowry calls Erskine's attention to this and other passages in Broch's essay in an unpublished letter of 14 October 1953 (U. B. C. Lowry collection).

25. *October Ferry to Gabriola,* ed. Margerie Lowry (New York and Cleveland: World, 1970), p. 210.

The problems Margerie Lowry confronted in preparing *October Ferry* for publication were essentially the same as those we have discussed in connection with *Dark as the Grave,* and most readers are likely to have the same reservations about her editorial procedures. A 1954 typescript with many marginal revisions in the author's hand constitutes the basis of the published text. She incorporates most of her husband's changes along with much material from his notes and alternate drafts. She also deletes and transposes passages on her own initiative and retains others that the artist had indicated were to be excised. The final page and a half of the book are taken, with only minor alterations, from the original short-story version of *October Ferry* that the two Lowrys had written together in 1946. The extent to which their collaboration continued beyond that point may be inferred from the following memorandum Lowry addressed to his wife: "How to *disentangle* the Tides of Eridanus section. In reality 3 separate versions exist, if not 4: *my* first; *your* revision of my first; *my* revision of your revision which put back most of what *you* cut out; and your impromptu version—an amalgam of the lot" (U. B. C. Lowry collection).

26. The McCandless was modeled on Lowry's friend Charles Stansfeld-Jones, a Welsh adept who had written two books on the Cabbala under the name Frater Achad. Stansfeld-Jones's library of works on magic and mysticism was the source of most of the information the novelist required for his depiction of the Consul's occultist side. See Day, *Malcolm Lowry,* pp. 294–95, and Kilgallin, *Lowry,* pp. 46–47, 51–52.

27. Freud makes the connection between eye symbolism and the Oedipus complex—"the blinding in the legend of Oedipus, as well as elsewhere, stands for castration"—in *The Interpretation*

of Dreams (*The Standard Edition of the Complete Psychological Works of Sigmund Freud*, trans. and ed. James Strachey et al. [London: Hogarth Press, 1953–74] 5:398). See also Freud's remarks on the anxiety caused by repressing masturbation (ibid., p. 586).

28. "It is [Ethan] and no one else that produces the so-called coincidences and disaster," declared Lowry; "himself, as it were, the paranoiac black magician of [his own and his family's] lives" (unpublished letter to Erskine, December 1953, U. B. C. Lowry collection).

29. Languishing in Sicily, unable to continue work on *October Ferry*, the novelist attempted to tell his Italian translator, Giorgio Monicelli, of his "ghastly incapacity to look [his] grief in the face": I fail... because I am still half unconvinced that it is not a Medusa that has to be grappled with from behind else I turn to stone" (draft of an unfinished 1955 letter, U. B. C. Lowry collection).

The theme of accountability for the death of another occurs in two unpublished works. The protagonist of the lost novel *In Ballast to the White Sea* "inadvertently... causes his brother to turn all his venom on himself in a Dostoievskian scene that leads to the brother's death" (*Letters*, p. 261). Gwyn, the brother, makes cameo appearances in several of Ethan's meditations in *October Ferry*, in which the latter blames himself for not having dissuaded the boy from undertaking a fatal voyage to Archangel. And in the fragment entitled *The Ordeal of Sigbjørn Wilderness* appears a character named Wensleydale whose suicide closely resembles that of Peter Cordwainer. The theme stems from Lowry's involvement in the death of Paul Fitte, one of his Cambridge classmates. See Kilgallin, pp. 18–19, and M. C. Bradbrook, *Malcolm Lowry* (London and New York: Cambridge Univ. Press, 1974), pp. 113–16, 161–62. A number of letters disputing the details of the Fitte case appear in the May 1974 issues of *TLS*.

30. Unpublished letter of December 1953 (U. B. C. Lowry collection).

31. Ibid.

32. *The Courage to Be* (New Haven: Yale Univ. Press, 1952), pp. 189–90.

33. Unpublished letter to Erskine, December 1953 (U. B. C. Lowry collection). For a more favorable estimate of the closing pages of *October Ferry* (and of the novel as a whole), see Terence Bareham, "After the Volcano: An Assessment of Malcolm Lowry's Posthumous Fiction," *Studies in the Novel* 6 (1974): 349–62, in which he asserts that the images are "beautifully worked out despite the 'edited' text" (p. 354). Bareham has, to my mind, confused the wish with the deed.

34. To Erskine, early summer 1953, *Letters,* p. 340.

35. 8 January 1953, *Letters,* p. 328.

36. To Cape, 2 January 1946, *Letters,* p. 59.

37. To Matson, 2 October 1951, *Letters,* p. 267.

38. Ibid., pp. 267–68. The other two stories named in this missive were "October Ferry" and "In the Black Hills," the second and third items respectively on the list. In an unpublished letter of 9 September 1952 (U. B. C. Lowry collection), the author describes *Hear Us O Lord* as having, like *Under the Volcano,* twelve "chapters"; however, he does not specify titles or indicate whether all of these pieces had actually been drafted.

39. *Letters,* p. 338. In this letter, written in early summer 1953, Lowry again speaks of twelve "chapters," the last four of which are named: "Ghostkeeper," "Pompeii," *October Ferry,* and "The Forest Path." *October Ferry* had by this time become, he remarks, "A short, perhaps even not so short novel.... Nonetheless I still have the hope it will fit into *Hear Us O Lord*" (p. 334).

40. See in particular the letters to David Markson of 1 November 1951 and spring 1956, *Letters,* pp. 269, 385.

41. *Malcolm Lowry: Psalms and Songs,* ed. Margerie Lowry (New York and Scarborough, Ont.: New American Library, 1975), p. 250. "Kristbjorg's Story: In the Black Hills" was first published, together with the early story "China," in pamphlet form by Aloe Editions (New York, 1974).

42. "In the Black Hills," p. 253.

43. A footnote to "Ghostkeeper" informs us that "this is not a 'finished' story, it is a first draft, with notes" (*Psalms and Songs,* p. 202. There is no reason to doubt this claim. The death of King George VI on 6 February 1952, which figures in "Ghostkeeper," and the author's reference to the story, in an unpublished letter to

Erskine of 20 March 1952, as one that he has recently written indicate the period of its composition.

44. The story was originally published together with a "A Memory of Malcolm Lowry," by C. G. McNeill, a Canadian physician, who recalls Margerie Lowry's having told him: "Malcolm dictates standing up. . . . He leans with the back of his hands on top of the desk. Sometimes he will stand that way for what seems an hour, thinking for the proper word. At the end of the day his legs are swollen and aching" (*American Review* 17 [May 1973]: 36). M. C. Bradbrook compares the oral effect of Lowry's dictation to ballads and seamen's yarns (*Malcolm Lowry*, p. 13).

45. To Erskine, May 1952, *Letters*, p. 320.

46. To Erskine, early summer 1953, *Letters*, p. 335.

47. See T. E. Bareham's discussion of linkage and development in *Hear Us O Lord* in "Strange Poems of God's Mercy," *The Art of Malcolm Lowry*, ed. Anne Smith (London: Vision Press, 1978), pp. 156-68.

48. "The force that through the green fuse drives the flower," *The Collected Poems of Dylan Thomas* (New York: New Directions, 1957), p. 10.

49. On the style of "Through the Panama," see Roger I. Yakoubovitch, "Cassure, canal, baranquilla," *Les lettres nouvelles* 2-3 (May-June 1974): 182-204.

50. To Erskine, *Letters*, p. 335. Writing to his agent Matson in November 1951, the novelist speaks of having "slugged out a rough version of. . .'Through the Panama' (later perhaps to be a chapter in one of the novels, here simply in the form of a journal, a sort of Arthur Gordon Pym)" (unpublished letter, U. B. C. collection).

51. In the first draft of *Dark as the Grave* the hero is called Martin Trumbaugh, and in the second and third, Sigbjørn Wilderness, the name he bears in the published version.

52. To Matson, 2 October 1951, *Letters*, p. 267.

53. Lowry considered the protagonist of "Strange Comfort" a different character from the Sigbjørn Wilderness of the other works (*Letters*, p. 327). Apart from his being an American and not having the house in Eridanus as an emotional anchor, however, the Sigbjørn of this story is virtually indistinguishable from

his namesake in *Dark as the Grave* or "Through the Panama."

54. *Letters,* pp. 20, 21.

55. "Why did I laugh tonight?" *The Poetical Works of John Keats,* ed. H. W. Garrod, 2nd ed. (Oxford: Clarendon, 1958), p. 470. On the relation between experimental modernism and a more traditional romanticism in Lowry's work, see Malcolm Bradbury, "Malcolm Lowry as Modernist," *Possibilities* (London and New York: Oxford Univ. Press, 1973), pp. 181–91.

56. Judging from the manuscripts at U. B. C., there is no piece in *Hear Us O Lord* in which the author invested more effort than "Elephant and Colosseum." The story went through a number of drafts and was the subject of a detailed critique by Margerie Lowry, which stressed the virtues of clarity, simplicity, and common sense. She wonders, for example, what exactly Cosnahan's magical powers have to do with his success as a writer. Again and again she pleads that passages which seem to her inflated or irrelevant be cut and, more often than not, she comes up against strong resistance from her husband. Some of the deletions she urged have in fact been made in the published version.

57. In an unpublished letter to Erskine of 14 October 1953, Lowry quotes the following passage from Broch's introduction to Hofmannsthal's *Selected Prose:* "nature, having been rendered harmless by culture and elevated to beauty, [has] in turn bequeathed to culture, as a permanent Greek gift, the sinister, the menacing" (p. xxviii).

58. To James Stern, 7 May 1940, *Letters,* p. 28. In December 1939 Conrad Aiken, after reading the manuscript of *In Ballast to the White Sea,* had advised Lowry to jettison "ghostly doppelgängers and projections and identifications and let loose some of your natural joy in swiftness and goodness and simplicity—put your complexity into reverse—and celebrate the sun" (*Selected Letters,* ed. Joseph Killorin [New Haven and London: Yale Univ. Press, 1978], p. 239).

59. *Correspondances,* in *Oeuvres complètes de Baudelaire,* ed. Y.-G. LeDantec and Claude Pichois (Paris: Pléiade, 1961), p. 11.

60. Barry Wood argues persuasively that the Tao, symbolizing opposites that grow out of or are defined by each other, is the "one image in the story which links together all [its] levels of

meaning" ("The Edge of Eternity," *Canadian Literature* 70 [autumn 1976]: 55).

61. *The Prelude,* ed. Ernest de Selincourt and Helen Darbishire, 2nd ed. (Oxford: Clarendon, 1959), p. 5 (bk. 1, lines 33, 41).

62. *Moby-Dick,* ed. Harrison Hayford and Hershel Parker (New York: Norton, 1967), p. 165.

63. In a letter to Erskine, written in Dollarton and dated 5 June 1951, Lowry comments: "Reading Dante the other day I came to the conclusion that the celestial scenery of pine trees and mountains inlet and sea here must be extremely like that in Ravenna where he...wrote and got inspiration for the last part of the *Paradiso.* Then I discovered that Eridanus in mythology among other things *is* the River Po and where the Po emerges to the sea *is* Ravenna. It gave me quite a turn, though I'm sure I don't see why it should have" (*Letters,* p. 245).

64. *Moby-Dick,* p. 444.

65. See Leon Howard's discussion of Melville's response to *Mosses from an Old Manse* in his *Herman Melville* (Berkeley and Los Angeles: Univ. of California Press, 1951), pp. 168ff.

66. *Go Down, Moses* (New York: Random House, 1942), p. 257. Wilderness declares, in "Through the Panama," that his principal affinities are with a "tradition of writers not English at all, but American...of which Faulkner and Aiken...are about the last living exponents" (H84).

67. *The Writings of Henry David Thoreau* (Boston and New York: Houghton Mifflin, 1906) 2:100.

68. In a letter to Erskine of early summer 1953, the novelist claims that *"Hear Us O Lord*...would be, if done aright,...a kind of—often far less serious, often much more so—*Volcano* in reverse, with a triumphant ending, but ending (after 'The Forest Path') in the same way, with the words Le Gusta Este Jardín" (*Letters,* p. 338).

69. The publisher's preface to *Hear Us O Lord* states: "[The author's] notes indicate that 'The Forest Path to the Spring' was a foreshadowing of one of the projected books, and that the final scene of 'The Forest Path' was to have been the final scene of the whole sequence" (H10). Day (*Malcolm Lowry,* p. 459) situates

this declaration of intent in a prospectus for the *Voyage* entitled *Work in Progress,* which Lowry sent to Matson on 22 November 1951. The novelist's plans for the *Voyage* were, as we have seen, fluid, and had he actually reached the point of conclusion he might well have composed a different scene. One can hardly imagine, though, that it would not have had some version of the *coincidentia oppositorum* as its center.

70. "Selige Sehnsucht," *Goethes Werke,* ed. Erich Trunz et al. (Hamburg: Wegner, 1948–60), 2:19.

Index